The Climb

Out of Grief, Into Joy

Rebecca Stanley

Table of Contents

Introduction 1

Chapter One - Origins 5

Chapter Two - The Incident 17

Chapter Three - Acceptance 31

Chapter Four - Forgiveness 43

Chapter Five - Surrender 67

Chapter Six - The Snag 87

Chapter Seven - The Scar 101

Chapter Eight - The Climb 109

The Prayer 121

Introduction

Dear Reader,

If you have picked up this book, I assume you are in a lot of pain or know someone who is. My heart goes out to you and I want you to know you are not alone. I wrote this book because I was given a gift that my mother and her mother never received. If it was offered to them, either they could not or would not accept it. My maternal grandparents' marriage ended in divorce. My grandmother died with a broken heart, stuck in her grief, always hoping that Granddad would reappear one day.

My mom divorced my dad and she, too, never recovered from her own deep sorrow. Mom tried fearlessly at times to break through the gray clouds of depression that kept her in the shadows, but she died with a heart full of grief over a past she could not go back and change. Neither my mom nor my grandmother ever took hold of the gift which would have enabled them to take the one step that might have made all the difference.

Years later, after my own divorce, I was offered this same gift, and by some miracle I was given the grace to receive it. I liken the gift to a long rope which appeared at the bottom of a dark hole in which I found myself. I could choose to grab the rope and start climbing, or I could just look at it, telling myself all the reasons why climbing it would not work: it's too long, I'm too weak, I'm too sad. Yet, an energy that was not my own propelled me to begin the climb out of the darkness of my grief and back into the light of joy, where my heart longed to live again.

This book is the story of my climb. It is not my story, as I never would have written it this way. This story was written by God and I am just the person telling it.

The climb was not easy and took longer than I thought it would. I needed help from others along the way. And though the climb hurt in places I was not prepared to hurt, it was still worth it, *so worth it* in the end.

One day I read this sentence, "Unforgiveness does not stop the pain. It spreads it." (A Grace Disguised: How the Soul Grows Through Loss, by Jerry Sittser, p.140). I then realized forgiveness was the rope I was offered, but it was up to me to make the climb. The theme of this story is forgiveness and how forgiveness stops the pain we are in.

My goal is not to make you think less of anyone in my story. I believe God loves everyone in my life as much as he loves me. My goal is to share with you what I learned while I put one foot in front of the other day after day. The lesson for me has been two-fold: God put my family in my life, not for me to change them, but for God to change me. And, forgiveness was the only acceptable response to the family members God used to chisel and shape my soul. Whatever has happened to cause you pain, perhaps this is how you will begin to see the events of your own life and view the people in your own story.

Godspeed!

1

Origins

Life was good long enough for me to remember the good days, only to mourn them when they were gone.

I often have mixed emotions after a trip to see Dad. It was always Dad and me as far back as my conscious memory will reach. Unlike Mom, he was the parent I related to the most. We were both early risers. He listened more than he talked. And his demeanor was the same day in and day out. On the other hand, Mom slept late and talked more. I was never sure what to expect on my first encounter with her each morning or when returning home from school. As a little girl, all I knew was that Dad just felt safer. Thus, my posture growing up was dadward and I have remained that way my whole life. Dad was also easier to converse with because he listened thoughtfully and asked questions. He was not the kind of dad who thought his opinion was the only correct one. This made it easier for me to form my own opinions. The one thing on which Dad never budged, however, were matters concerning God. I was allowed to question what we as a family believed, but Dad never wavered on his answers. His certainty gave me a confidence I didn't appreciate until much later in life.

On my way home from Dad's, I reflect on our conversations that take place on his porch overlooking the back yard. We are frequently interrupted by the chatter of the birds which hover around Dad's well stocked feeders. When the squirrels show up, Dad cheers for the birds, while I sit quietly relieved for the squirrels that his porch now has glass windows that no longer accommodate the bb gun still lying next to his chair. To this day, no topic of conversation is off limits. Always in the queue are sermon ideas, the grandkids, world events, and the calls he still receives from people in positions of leadership around the country. However, my favorite discussions center around what we are both learning personally. Scattered throughout the day is lots of humor, *we think we're funny*! And in the evenings before bedtime we pray, dad still gets on his knees. Listening to Dad talk to God does more to increase my faith than witnessing a miracle. Just like when I was a little girl, if Dad prays about something, I *know* God is paying attention.

During the flight home, it's hard to resist the temptation to mourn my childhood again. So many good memories stirred in with the bad. My thoughts invariably go to the question of "why." Why couldn't Mom and Dad's marriage have made it? Why couldn't Mom, who was so beautiful, gifted, vibrant, and well loved by many, climb out of her childhood dysfunction, and thrive in the life she had with the family she loved? I never doubted my parents' love for each other, and I don't believe they did either. Inevitably, I struggle not to blame God.

Dad put family first. Though he was busy being the pastor of the First Baptist Church in Miami, Florida, then Bartow, Florida and finally Atlanta, Georgia, he was available when I needed him. One of my favorite childhood memories was touring our neighborhood in Miami on the handlebars of his bike just as the sun began to rise. Dad and I were the early birds, and in the mornings, I knew just where to find him. If he wasn't in his study, I would gather up the hem of my nightgown and run across the dew-covered grass of our backyard to his prayer room, a converted tool shed. I could hear him before I could see him. On opening the door, I would find him stretched out on the afghan that Becca, his mom, made for him. His Bible was always open with a handkerchief close by. No matter how focused he was at that moment, he never seemed to mind my interruption. I only had to say, "Can we go now, Dad?"

Settled above the front tire, my nightgown wrapped around my legs, we would ride through the quiet streets singing "Raindrops on roses and whiskers on kittens, bright copper kettles and warm woolen mittens…"

Dad's example has stayed with me my whole life. Everywhere I moved, I would first stake out a place to be alone with God in the mornings. I grew up knowing if you talk to God, He will eventually talk back. And the more you listen, the more He will say. The only condition is obedience.

Dad was the introvert, and Mom was the extrovert. Mom embodied the cliché, "I never met a stranger." She claimed her gift was mercy, but as a child, I thought her gift was talking. She could turn a quick errand into an hour-long conversation with anyone from the sales lady to the gas station attendant. If she was the perpetual talker, I was the perpetual *waiter.* These constant encounters bothered me because I never felt I held her attention as other people did. Mom seemed to be on a mission, it just didn't include me.

Maybe it was the early tremors of her own brokenness that attracted Mom to individuals others might overlook. She had an instinct about people, and once she engaged them, she would unapologetically share Christ with them, and many inevitably became believers. Our life-long babysitter, Virginia, was a prime example. A nineteen-year-old student when Mom first met her, Virginia's home life was difficult, if not dangerous. Mom shared Christ with Virginia and made it clear that should she need a safe place to land, she could walk through our door and feel at home. I know now this is how I formed such a strong attachment to Virginia. Her homelife must have been awful, as she was with us almost all the time.

Virginia was just one in a long line of single women Mom mentored throughout her life. I admit to feeling ignored and frustrated with her over the lengthy phone conversations with brokenhearted single women who called for advice. Inevitably their troubles revolved around men. Mom, who hardly spent any time being a single adult herself, mixed mercy and truth, as she confidently counseled these young women about what the Bible taught regarding purity and the assurance of God's love and forgiveness.

Another attribute making Mom a perfect fit for Dad was her gift of hospitality. Not only could she set a lovely table on a tight budget, but her roast beef on Sunday afternoons rivaled any Michelin star restaurant. Rarely just the four of us, we dined with everyone from missionaries, to church members, to lonely singles who needed a home cooked meal. Mom treated all our guests the same. And meals weren't just about the delicious fare, how the napkins were folded, or whether the biscuits rose. The conversations during our meals held equal billing. As all Mom and Dad's friends knew, my parents didn't waste time on trivia. Dispensing with small talk, our family broke the 'rules' and openly discussed politics and religion – especially theology.

Mom's knowledge of the Bible rivaled Dad's, and she never hesitated to correct him. Her memory was equally phenomenal, and she could produce the most remote Bible verse to support her argument. Dad never seemed to mind.

Many nights Virginia and I were left doing the dishes while Mom retreated to the study with Dad while he worked on his Sunday sermon. They were a team. Despite my own frustrations with Mom, she and dad seemed to fit perfectly together, until they didn't.

Just as with Bible knowledge, Mom and Dad's parenting was also in sync. Though Dad talked for a living and Mom just loved to talk, they used their words sparingly in raising Andy, my brother, and me. Neither of them placed importance on yelling or scolding in the face of wrongdoing. When we were young, they let the paddle do the talking. When we were older, and it came to advice on matters, they did not offer much unless we asked for it, and even then, their words were measured. Their quiet confidence in Andy and me probably did more to shape our character than anything, and I believe they saw this as more effective than a lecture on how far *not* to go in the back seat of a car on Friday night.

Make no mistake, however. We knew where Mom and Dad stood on most things. And for some reason, we had no desire to go against them. I think it was partly because we never doubted their bedrock love for us. *I just enjoyed Dad's love more.* Unlike the monologues I endured from Mom, my conversations with Dad went both ways. He listened as if I had something important to say. He could be stern but was never mean. Though Dad stood large in our psyche, the other reason Andy and I never rebelled was that *his relationship with God stood even larger.* His habit of always pointing us to God, like a compass pointing north, was a constant reminder of to whom we were truly accountable. *At some point Dad must have also driven home the fact that God is everywhere.*

Dad's sayings, like "Obey God and leave all the consequences to Him," and "To succeed in life you must be willing to sacrifice the present for the future" were his way of letting us know what he thought. Rather than charge at us like the calvary in the old westerns we watched as a family, Dad just kept repeating the truths *he* lived by and, somehow, they took hold.

Anyone who knew Mom well knew her creativity kicked in at nighttime. She would stay up into the early hours only to sleep most of the next day. At night, if I could not find her, I always knew where to look. She was in the basement working on a project, like spray-painting bird's nests for party favors for the deacons at Christmas, or in her tiny study preparing for her Sunday School lesson, or she was in her closet.

Mom's closet was sacred, and one did not enter unless one was beckoned, including Dad. Some of the few conversations we had which I actually enjoyed, were our visits with me standing at the door of her closet watching her organize her shoe boxes. With the same reverence she displayed while teaching a book of the Old Testament, Mom taught me about wool versus cotton, tailored versus trendy, and how to tell if a dress was well made. "Always check the hem," she would say. I listened intently to these lessons and tucked them away with the same importance she placed on them. Mom took her appearance seriously, so I did too. At least it was something we had in common. I was desperate to have something, *anything*, in common with a mom I didn't understand, rarely enjoyed, mostly resented, but was dying to be noticed by. For once *I* wanted to be in her spotlight receiving the love and attention she gave to everyone else.

When I was about 11 years old, I discovered a time during the week I could be with Dad without any interruptions. On Sunday mornings, I arose and dressed early to be ready when he left for church. My goal was to be in the car when he backed out of our driveway. The first thing we did was turn the radio to Peach 94.9 and sing along to the hymn that was playing.

Nothing meant as much to me as having Dad all to myself on that thirty-minute drive to church. Knowing that Sundays were "go-days" for Dad I wanted to be relevant, so I asked the obvious question, "What are you preaching on today, Dad?" And our discussion would begin. He would start by telling me the scripture and points on his outline and then would turn to me and ask, "What do you think, Beck?" I knew he meant it, so I would plunge in, giving my two cents worth. He listened to me as if I was a seminary professor telling him something he had never considered. *And occasionally he hadn't!* Those rides to church with Dad made me feel like I was a part of what Dad did. I felt as if we all were a part of something bigger than ourselves. As if we were headed toward a specific destiny with a momentum over which we had no control. Even then God was writing our story, it just wasn't the one we thought He would tell.

With our move to Atlanta, the wind began to shift in our family. Everything was bigger. The church Dad worked at was bigger, Andy's and my schools were bigger, and there were more people's names to remember. The ride to church was longer than ten minutes, unlike the small town of Bartow where we could walk or ride our bikes everywhere. Professionally, Dad faced difficult challenges at work, and suddenly people who we thought were our friends would not speak to us anymore. While Dad took on more responsibility at church, Mom retreated deeper into depression. She either stayed in bed longer or stayed away from home more often. All the energy she used to have for people and projects seemed to gradually drain away. I was left to do the housework, put away the groceries, clean the dishes after supper, and anything else Mom didn't feel like doing. No one asked me if I wanted this role. It felt like I was demoted to servitude. *I had become Cinderella, but not the princess, just the help.*

In the beginning of Mom's decline, she still taught Sunday school to single adults and was greatly admired for her knowledge and ability to communicate. But after a while her teaching stopped too.

Though the tremors in Mom's emotional health occurred more often, we still took family vacations which drew us back together, at least for a little while. Dad always made those trips a priority. One time, we camped in a trailer traveling all the way to California and back. At every campsite, Andy and I would go in search of new friends, while Mom and Dad connected the utilities and prepared dinner. At night, we played Rook for hours, Dad and I usually on a team against Mom and Andy. Sometimes, we would sit by the fire and listen to Andy strum his guitar and sing. I love those memories because out there under the stars it felt like all was well with the world. But with each arrival home, *our* world was a little less certain and a lot more troubled.

By the time I was in high school, Dad was rising in prominence while Mom's descent continued. As a teenager, I struggled to reconcile the faith we had and the life we lived with the highs and lows that were occurring more often. *What was wrong with Mom? Why couldn't Dad fix it?* Many a night I found myself crying tears of anger and frustration on my friend Martha's sofa when I felt I couldn't take life at home anymore.

2

The Incident

"Consider what God has done: Who can straighten what he has made crooked? When times are good, be happy; but when times are bad consider that God has made the one as well as the other. Therefore, a man cannot discover anything about his future."

Ecclesiastes 7:13-14

The last two years of our marriage my husband, James, was sending me a message. I could hear his words, but I didn't comprehend his meaning. In our arguments, his new phrase, "Just leave if you're so unhappy!" began to surface more often. Happiness had stopped being a consideration a long time ago. I was in survival mode. So I would respond, "I'm not going anywhere." I was in our marriage for the long haul and I meant it, regardless of how secretly unhappy I was. *It wasn't a secret. My friends knew long before I told them.*

Then rudeness began to replace the sparse kindness that was left in our marriage. His tone of voice was perpetually agitated. We rarely made eye contact. He would hole up in his office every night with the doors shut. I heard *that* message, loud and clear, but I didn't mind. *If I'd had doors to shut, I would have shut mine too.*

The year before our last summer together, he began a public relations campaign against me using the children. Suddenly, the children's demeanor toward me began to mirror his. I didn't understand what was happening, except I knew the more time my kids spent with their dad, the more distant they were from me. They began to question everything I said and lobbed criticisms at me out of nowhere. This cut deep in places I was not prepared to hurt. My children's behavior toward me exposed how I had come to depend on their love and acceptance, in the absence of my husband's. Now I saw cracks forming between us as well. My hope for a happily-ever-after was disappearing before my eyes. My prayers felt hollow as I struggled to know how to pray. I clung to my theology about God, what I knew to be true about Him. But with every hurtful comment, I felt even more lonely and desperate.

It didn't take a counselor to tell me my daily Bible reading and routine prayers were not going to fix this problem. I had yet to be honest with myself over the fact that I had kept God at a safe, comfortable distance for most of my life, *that would come later.* I truly believed, but He wasn't someone I spent more time with than necessary. Now I needed Him to come fix my family. I needed Him to do what I knew only He could do, *if He would.* I needed a miracle. I was too afraid to ask, but I asked anyway. Afraid of the answer and the disappointment that might send me into oblivion, I begged, daily, *"Please don't let me down like You did mom and dad."* Surely that was not where this was headed. It just couldn't be. *Not again.*

The summer my daughter, Sarah, was due with her first baby, my husband took our two sons on a trip to Europe *we* had planned to take together. Sarah had taken up much of the family's attention the year before, but now that she was married, it was time to do something with just the boys before they graduated from college. I, especially, felt the need to reconnect with them. Since Sarah was due in early August and our trip was planned for June, I hoped this was time enough to travel and return. But James didn't want me to go and was making it perfectly clear. Every chance he had, he would say, "You don't have to go, you don't need to go," which translated to "I don't want you to go." I finally took the 'hints' and decided to stay home. My first son had arrived two weeks early, *what if Sarah took after me?*

I was sad and angry the whole time they were gone. I felt cheated. I *had* been cheated out of time away with my sons on the brink of their independence and manhood. Was I overreacting or simply scared this was more manipulation to drive a wedge between my children and me? I felt helpless and so hopelessly frustrated. Using them against me wasn't fair. It wasn't right. I couldn't fight my husband's addiction, and he seemed more interested in battling me than the thing that was about to destroy us. How was I to survive this without becoming an addict myself? It was actually too late. I was already one. I was addicted to changing what I thought I could change, but I was told I couldn't by my friends in Al-Anon. This *was* insanity.

The trip to Europe was a disaster. I received middle of the night calls from both sons throughout the trip. I was listening, and what I heard was hurt, anger, and disappointment. *"I know how you feel," I wanted to say, but didn't. How to validate them, without criticizing their dad? I tried, but I wasn't always successful.*

On their arrival home, James worked hard to convince me how great their trip had been. But his words had stopped mattering to me. I had little to no regard for him anymore. Honestly, I loathed him for taking the boys to Europe and ruining their trip with more of his irresponsible behavior. *Be as rude to me as you want to, but hurt my sons and I don't care about you anymore.* Knowing it was wrong to feel that way, I couldn't change how I felt. I was stuck between the proverbial rock and a hard place. I couldn't stand the man I was married to, though I wasn't ready to use the word hate. I wanted him to want help, and then go get it. I wanted him to love me and the children more than his addiction. I wanted him to do whatever it took to save our family. But I couldn't make him. Every week in Al-Anon, I heard this phrase, "You didn't cause it, you can't change it, and you can't cure it." *I know that!* But I wanted to stomp my feet and scream, "STOP IT, STOP IT, STOP IT!" anyway.

So, there we were, two miserable people "trapped," *his word,* in a self-destructive relationship because we were both in survival mode, which no one can sustain for long without breaking down. As neither of us was being authentic, we were mutually lonely. And we were desperate because there seemed to be no acceptable way out. Divorce had never been an option. We never even mentioned it in our most heated arguments. "Leave" had become his code word for it, but I kept ignoring that.

On the fourth of July, we had some out-of-town friends over for a barbeque. After dinner we planned to drive about twelve blocks from our house to a fireworks show. When it was time to leave, I was prepared to drive with car keys in hand. James insisted on driving. Knowing where that argument would lead, I chose to ride with Sarah and her husband in their car. James left first, while we followed from behind. As I sat in the back seat I quietly prayed that God would please protect James and everyone else around him.

I couldn't sleep that night after witnessing firsthand that James' problem had become a matter of life and death. The next morning I called our Sunday school teacher and nervously asked if I could come over. Outside of my two best friends, I had not told anyone about James. Broadening that safe circle frightened me. I feared what telling our Sunday school teacher might trigger. The outcome could go one of two ways. James, on being confronted, would agree to receive help; or, he would become angrier, and refuse help. Would it end our marriage? There wasn't much "marriage" left to our relationship. My friends in Al-Anon would remind me that I couldn't control his reaction, and it would be crazy to try, I could only control mine. Even so, I had to do whatever I could to stop the madness.

So, the next day I sat on the edge of my Sunday school teacher's sofa and poured my heart out. Telling Mark, and his wife, Hannah, was difficult, but not as difficult as I thought. Mark said he would call James to talk. Relieved but still nervous, I thanked them and left. Predictably, James came home furious with me after he met with Mark. He hid in his office the entire evening with a book which Mark had given him to read. We avoided each other the rest of the summer until Sarah's baby arrived July 29th. Sarah wanted her husband and me in the room when she gave birth. Witnessing the birth of our first grandson was a miracle I wanted to share with James, but never did. At the hospital he would not look at me. He came and went as if it was no big deal.

August ninth, that summer, James came home and picked a fight with our youngest son, Luke. It started at dinner and ended up in Luke's room with the door closed. The memory of those phone calls from Europe were still fresh in my mind, so I opened the door to Luke's room and calmly said, "There's no one home but the three of us so why not leave the door open." The details of the incident that followed are not necessary for the purpose of my story. I will only share that my son and I fled our home that night and I never lived under the same roof with James again.

My friend Betty, and her husband, let us stay with them for the weekend. Her husband connected me with an attorney who helped me with the paperwork to put a restraining order in place. At the insistence of my friend, Lauren, I filed a police report and had pictures made of my injuries. I then called our business partner's wife and asked if she could meet me. We met at a restaurant and I told her everything as we both wept. She needed to know, because whatever happened next might impact her and her husband and I wanted them to be prepared. They were not just business acquaintances, but dear friends.

Overnight my life had taken a horrible turn leaving me in unfamiliar territory. Everything seemed uncertain. Everything except God, but strangely, at that moment, not even He felt safe. I didn't understand addiction. I had no idea it becomes the most important thing in a person's life – even more important than a wife and three children who love you with all their hearts and desperately need your love in return. Surely there had been a mistake and I had been dropped into someone else's life. This could *not* be my story. My body ached all over and I longed to escape its confines. Shame engulfed me. I didn't want to be around people. *I didn't want to be alone with me.* I could not see any good coming out of this. I only saw the pain in my children's eyes, and a confused and frightened woman who I didn't recognize when I looked in the mirror.

A year and two months after the incident in August, I stood in a courtroom while the judge's gavel went down as she announced that James and I were officially divorced. I went home in shock and sat in my living room alone. The battle was over. Nobody won. I was exhausted. But more than that, I was afraid. I had no idea what to do next.

I knew how to be a wife, a mom, a daughter and a friend, but I had no idea how to be divorced. For years I wasn't friends with any divorced people. Divorce was a stigma, a disease, and I didn't want to get close enough to anyone to catch it. The divorced women I knew of had lives I did not envy. Most struggled financially and their kids weren't necessarily well behaved. From where I stood, they wore perpetual frowns and walked around with a chip on their shoulders. When they spoke, it was impossible not to notice the grudge they held against men. I didn't think I had any thing in common with these women and more importantly, I didn't want to.

Then suddenly, on a Wednesday morning in October, I became a member of their club. For the rest of my life, I would circle the "D" on medical forms and applications. Could this really be my fate? Lying awake at night, picturing my wedding day, I remembered Dad turning to me saying "Are you sure about this?" just before we entered the church. No, I actually had not been sure. Was it me or marriage that I doubted most? I don't know. If Dad and Mom couldn't stay married, how did I think I was going to? If Dad had told me right then and there, "Beck, I don't have a good feeling about this," I would have turned around and run. But fourteen hundred people were waiting, so I said, "Yes," and off we went down the aisle.

What I could not reconcile was if my marriage was going to end in divorce, why didn't God prevent it from happening in the first place? How could God allow a marriage that began with two words "I do," in a church, end twenty-six years later with those same two words in a courtroom when I was asked if I understood what the judge was saying? Betrayal, defiance and a demand for justice ran through my veins in a way that frightened me. Suddenly I was demanding answers to questions I had never had the courage to ask, "Why does God let bad things happen if He has the power to stop it?" He's either good, but powerless. Or He's bad with power. Which is it? *I'm embarrassed to admit that many mornings in place of the time when I quietly prayed about the day ahead and read something inspirational, instead I beat my hands against the chest of a God who I knew loved me with a love I could not understand at the moment, and Who I hoped could handle my rebel heart.*

In the May preceding the 4th of July debacle, our family visited our previous hometown in Florida. Little did I suspect it was to be the last vacation for the five of us together. The first day, Sunday, was Mother's Day and the minister's message was from the book of Matthew, chapter 4, when Jesus began calling his disciples to follow Him. As I sat listening intently to this familiar story, I heard another voice in my head. It said, "Becky, something is going to happen, and I want you to follow Me closely." It was as real as the minister's voice, and I knew it was God.

Throughout the summer, I thought about those words and wondered when something would happen. My youngest son was leaving for college in the Fall and I thought that perhaps I might become more involved in our business. In some way, I wanted to reach out and help the women who worked for us. Never mind that our marriage was hanging by a thread, I only had positive thoughts about what God might be up to. It never occurred to me that something tragic was about to occur. *Never.* Instead of the peace I longed for, the hope I had for James pursuing help, and the faith I had that our marriage could heal, I was thrust into a war I had no desire to fight. Every day, during our divorce, I can honestly say, I prayed that God would stop the battles. I prayed James would come to his senses regarding his behavior, own it, apologize, and be willing to take steps toward real change. But in August, after the restraining order was in place, James and I were prevented from having face to face conversations. And after reading the multiple texts he sent me many an evening I was glad I did not have to endure one.

One morning after the divorce was final, I came across this conversation in John 6 between the disciple Peter and Jesus: "At this point many of his disciples turned away and deserted him. Then Jesus turned to the twelve and asked, 'Are you also going to leave?' Simon Peter replied, 'Lord, to whom would we go? You have the words that give eternal life. We believe, and we know you are the holy one of God.'" (John 6:66-69, The New Living Bible Translation)

I was at that "point", too, with Jesus. Life was not going to be the happily ever after story that I had expected. Following Jesus had just become a lot harder. Nothing about my life made sense except the decision I made when I was five years old. Seated in the second row of our church, while drawing pictures on tithing envelopes, I had listened to hundreds of sermons. I understood Jesus died for me and rose from the dead three days later so I could live with Him forever in heaven. I never doubted it for a moment. And I never doubted the decision I made one morning before kindergarten, asking God to forgive my sins and to please send Jesus into my heart. Dad prayed with me, as we knelt beside my bed and wept happy tears.

Oh how I wanted to put that little girl on my lap and warn her. But she would not have understood, just like I could not understand now. With fragile faith and an even more fragile peace, I prayed my version of Peter's answer, "Lord, You are all I have, though I am not sure if You even like me anymore. Am I in trouble with You because I divorced my husband and damaged my children's trust in all things good? I tried my hardest, and I failed at the most important relationship in life. I'm nothing. I'm no good. I want to disappear. I don't deserve to know You, and I'm not sure if I trust You anymore. I know You are God, but are You still good? So-what if I go to heaven when I die, what about today? And tomorrow? Where's the path I was on? I feel completely lost. Amen."

3

Acceptance

"No man knows how bad he is until
he has tried very hard to be good."

C.S. Lewis, Mere Christianity.

The reason Jesus requests His followers to give up everything for His sake, is because He gave up everything for ours. Even today, many Muslims understand the price of their decision to follow Christ better than we who are outside the Muslim faith. A Muslim can be disowned by his father and entire family for becoming a Christian. Early in their faith, they *have* to count the cost of what it means to follow Jesus, and sometimes they *do* lose everything.

While at a high school church-camp, I rededicated my life to Christ, saying, "I'm all in, Lord. Not my will, but Yours be done," and I meant it with all my heart. On arriving home, I told Dad of my recommitment, and he was proud of me. Instead of shame, there was praise and encouragement. I was certain my decision meant my life would turn out not just well, but exceptionally well. Planning to take my relationship with God seriously for the rest of my life, I thought, automatically set me up for success. *I never counted the costs of this decision, I didn't think there would be any.*

With the failure of both of our parents' marriages in the rearview mirror, I assumed James and I were equally motivated to avoid their same mistakes. We planned to carve out a different future for our new family. A future that avoided pain, and in which failure was not an option. We would live happily ever after and so would our children.

Surely my plan lined up with God's and He would help me execute it. However, my thinking was flawed. I didn't know my own heart, but God did. Rather than see my way clear, I was blind to the sin that needed to be excavated and removed. The kind of happily ever after that lead from one mountain top to the next, would have left me weak, coddled, ineffective and uncaring about those who God wanted me to care about. Instead, God led me through a long valley that felt much like the wilderness. Years later, I discovered a man who fundamentally changed my thinking about the value of the lower roads-the place where God removes the things that will destroy us with the precision of a surgeon who lovingly saves a patient's life. (Timothy Keller, "A Christian's Happiness")

In the beginning stages of the divorce I did everything possible to save money. I was paying the attorneys mounds of it and I didn't know how long it would last. Having sold our home, I moved into a small apartment in a high rise in a different part of town. I was not interested in making new friends. *Hi, I'm Becky, the new cliché in the building. I'm getting divorced. My children don't speak to me. But come see the new fern I bought for my balcony.*

Normally an avid reader, I could no longer focus on a sentence, much less a page in a book. Since my family started attending a Presbyterian church, I had come to discover a whole new world of Presbyterian ministers with whom I was not familiar. So occasionally I listened to them, primarily out of curiosity. I became a fan of one in particular because of his love for C.S. Lewis. His name was Dr. Tim Keller and he had a church called Redeemer in New York City. Discovering he had several series of free sermons online, I began to listen to him on my daily walks.

Late afternoons were the loneliest hours for me. For twenty-six years I had cooked dinner most nights, and suddenly I had no one to cook for and no appetite to speak of. To fill the space, I traded my favorite playlist, apron, and the aroma of onions and garlic, for sneakers, sidewalks with the hustle of five o'clock traffic, and Keller's next podcast I hoped would bring clarity, peace, and healing to my broken heart. One evening I found a sermon called "A Christian's Happiness" about Romans 8:28. Having memorized that verse in high school, I thought I knew its meaning, but decided to listen to his explanation and see if he had anything *new* to say. By the time his message was over, I was crying uncontrollably, and I was more than two miles away from home. So I listened again, and again, and again.

This was the start of a long and meaningful relationship with a mentor who I have never met. During those years of life in 17F, my apartment number, I listened to almost all of his free sermons multiple times. When I became employed and received my first paycheck, I sent part of my tithe to Redeemer. It was the least I could do. In "A Christian's Happiness", Keller clarified an error in my theology about suffering. Until then, I didn't have a category for suffering. I never intended to go through it. Suffering was for those outside the United States. Brokenness was for people like Dad, those on the front lines of Christianity who were making the enemy especially angry. It was my intention to fly under the radar of suffering. But my current situation told me God had something else in mind.

Keller began his message with this sentence, "There is a joy available that the deepest trouble can't put out, and if properly nourished and properly nurtured, it can co-exist with and even overwhelm the greatest grief." This got my attention. Joy had eluded me for years. Worry, doubt, and fear were my companions. Joy seemed hidden behind a dense mist. I knew it existed, just not for me.

According to Keller, to the degree that we understand Romans 8 is the degree to which we will experience an "impervious and relentless" joy. Those two words rolled over my *impervious* brain, as I thought, *"You don't know what I've just been through. I'm incapable of joy right now."*

He made three points: "The bad things turn out for good, the good things cannot be lost, and the best things are yet to come." These are the reasons for a Christian's joy.

The radical shift for me was in the discussion of his first point. "Our bad things turn out for good." Keller said that Romans 8:28 actually says, "To those loving Him, God works together all things for good." I always thought the verse meant all things will *be* good for those who follow Christ and do the right thing.

But Keller's point was "all things happen to Christians." "Experience shows us that all the same things that happen to everybody else will happen to those who love God," he said. *"All* things" means *"all* things!" I needed it repeated several times because I could still not accept that "all things" included my divorce and my brokenhearted family.

This was a real contradiction for me. I had been convinced that my life circumstances would and *should* be a little better than those who did not believe like I did. Didn't following the rules have its merits? Didn't God favor those who obeyed Him with His blessings? Don't we carry a little weight when it comes to the direction of our lives by our obedience and belief?

Keller had more evidence for his argument than I had for mine. Because the world is burdened down with sin, it's the nature of things to disintegrate, like the mountains which turn into the tiny grains of sand on the beach. Things do not come together, and they do not work together on their own. And if and when things *do* work together for good in your life, it is because of God. "If anything is going well," he said, "it's God's doing," *not ours.*

What I was hearing was that I have very little control over the outcomes of my life. Does nothing I do matter? I found this disconcerting. Even more troubling, his message unveiled a long-held distrust I had toward God. I had been holding a grudge against God for what happened to my parents. In my mind, no two people wanted to do God's will more than Mom and Dad. Why had He let their marriage fail? If that was His decision, what was good about it? And now Keller was telling me that it was only God's doing when things *do* work together. Why didn't God work to keep Mom and Dad together? They saw counselors, read their Bibles, and prayed continuously. And no one was unfaithful. Shouldn't they have succeeded?

Keller went on to say that the promise to believers is not better circumstances. The promise is a better life. *What kind of better life?* The bad things *are* bad. But He will bring good from the bad to bless you. The death of Lazarus is one of Keller's examples. Jesus stood at the tomb of Lazarus angry and weeping. (John 11:38) Why? Because it was a terrible thing. Death is terrible, loneliness is terrible, pain is terrible, *divorce is terrible.* "Jesus hates it (sin) so much that He was willing to come into this world so He could eventually destroy it (sin) without destroying us," said Keller.

If you love God, more good things will happen is not the promise. No! God will work the bad for good in the totality of your life. But, Keller said, don't give God a week, or a month or even a year or a decade, however. "The promise is, that taken in the totality of all of your life and the whole of everything God promises if you love Him, He will make sure it works for good."

Initially, I thought this point was a cop out. An inadequate excuse for God having allowed sincere believers' lives to fall apart while not coming to their rescue. Surely that was not an effective strategy to attract an unbelieving world. Shouldn't the flow of a believer's life course differently than a non-believer's?

Having extended my walk because of the anxiety I was feeling over Keller's arguments, he then made this statement: "Everything is necessary that He sends, nothing can be necessary that He withholds."

He explained it like this, "The premise is, the things that really hurt you and really kill you are foolishness, pride, selfishness, hardness of heart, denial of your flaws and weaknesses, and the belief that you don't need God." Those are the things that can hurt you in the long run, he argued. "Those are the only things that can hurt you in the totality of your life." Without warning, pent up tears began to pour down my cheeks, as the hard, frozen parts of my heart slowly began to thaw.

Suddenly I was awake to the realization that I was guilty of everything on that list. It was *my* heart that needed radical transformation to occur this whole time. *I'm* the one who thought I had Christianity by the tail and was going to wield my life where I wanted it to go. These were the sins God was trying to purge from *my* heart, but I couldn't hear Him because I was too busy pointing my finger at someone else.

"And the bad things God hates, God will allow, only in order to cure you from the things that can really destroy you," added Keller. The divorce was not a punishment? The harm done to me was not a mistake? It was the result of the fallen world I live *and* participate in? But rather than shame me for it, God was using it to bring good into my life by removing the sin in my heart that kept me from being completely His? *It felt too good to be true.*

Throughout the truly bad things He had allowed, God had been in control, and what He wanted was for me to relinquish my control. The bad things weren't rejection! They were God's invitation! *Hadn't he whispered, "Follow me closely"?*

Then Keller said, "The good things we have cannot be lost." Once my eyes were opened to understanding pain and loss as instruments for good, not careless punishments wielded by an angry parent, there was no turning back for me. I was able to accept what happened in my parents' marriage and my own marriage as a gift. A friend of mine once said, "Becky, you didn't ask for it, but you've been given a gift in a black box." She was right. And God's intention is for His gifts to multiply in our lives so that others reap the benefits too.

This may not be the last black box I receive. Life rolls in and out of seasons. But to Keller's point, our "Christian happiness," our joy, can remain constant and impervious throughout our lives because it is not based on our circumstances, but on the unfailing love of Jesus and His lifelong commitment to us and to our good. Whatever comes next, I may not want it, *or think I need it,* but I cannot with any integrity question God's motive for sending it. I will do my best to adopt C.S. Lewis' attitude, "I'll do what you say, I'll accept what you send."

Once I was able to accept that God could *love* me and *hate* divorce, the anger and bitterness I had toward my husband felt out of place in my heart. How could the love of Jesus and the hatred of man co-exist inside me? Learning to accept God's love in my current condition gave me the foundation I needed to let go of my bitterness and begin to forgive.

4

Forgiveness

"Beware, the person you like least, may
end up being you."

C.S. Lewis via Tim Keller's, Forgiveness

On October 8, 2014 I was officially no longer a married woman, but I didn't have much time to ponder my new identity. Three weeks later I was trick-or-treating with my grandsons and I received a call from Andy telling me to come home, mom was in the hospital. I booked a flight to Atlanta for the next day, planning to spend two nights with Mom. I had a commitment the following week that I needed to return for. I ended up cancelling the commitment and the flight, because twelve days later we buried her. It was completely unexpected. Mom always had an ailment of some kind, but she was generally healthier than she wanted to admit. Putting her in the hospital for a cough just hadn't seemed that serious. The day before she died, my dad came to the hospital, and for the first time in twenty years the four of us, Dad, Andy, Mom and I were all in the same room together. Just us. Andy and I were kids again, I could tell he felt it too. Dad told mom he loved her, then we all held hands and Dad led us in prayer, just like the family pow-wow's we use to have when we were little. The ones where we made decisions as a family like, how much to give to a certain need, where to go on vacation, and do we get a puppy or not? I wish I could hold on to that moment forever. When it was time to leave, I cried all the way to Dad's house, partly over Mom, and partly over my own children who now carried the same scars I had. *Oh God, how are you going to turn this for good?*

After the holidays, my close friend and mentor, Martha called me one day and said, "Becky, I think you have a bitter root judgment against your mom." I wasn't sure what a "bitter root judgment" was but I said, "Yes, I think you're right. And she's not the only one." In her adult years Martha realized that she had carried bitterness and unforgiveness toward her father since she was a teenager. In her efforts to forgive her father she had taken the principles of dealing with a bitter root judgment and formed a prayer that she used to walk through the process of forgiveness. Over the years she had changed the prayer to fit the different needs and circumstances of her clients, but the overall principle had remained the same. She sent me her version of the prayer as a map so that I could work through it and make it my own.

I desperately needed help because since Mom's death people would say to me, "I'm sorry to hear about your mom, you must really miss her." In response I would lie and say, "Yes, thank you." The more people expressed their sympathy the more I realized I wasn't sad over Mom, I was actually furious at her. I hardly remembered Mom in my childhood years. I have no memories of her reading me a book or of days doing nothing together. She just wasn't there. When I had my own children I wanted to be different. I wasn't the hovering kind of parent, but I made it a point to be present when I was with them. *Please don't read into this that I think I was better than Mom. I wasn't, I just tried not to make the same mistakes she did. Instead, I made plenty of my own.*

Virginia came into our lives when I was eight months old. Since she lived with her mom and an abusive stepdad, she spent as much time with us as she could. Virginia became my emotional attachment in life and I loved her more than I loved Mom, mostly because she was present. VA, as Dad called her, was funny, and she told entertaining stories. She was also a good listener and acted like what I had to say mattered. When Mom and Dad were gone for weeks at a time in the summers, Virginia came. And when she left I had terrible separation anxiety and would mourn her absence for days. She eventually became a teacher in Tennessee, which enabled her to spend summers and most holidays with us. Even into our teenage and adult years Virginia was present.

Mom never seemed to mind the role Virginia played in my life. When Virginia showed up, it was as if Mom resigned her job and left the building. Then one morning she actually did.

I was in seventh grade. Breakfast was over and Dad was in his study, while Andy and I were upstairs getting ready for school. Suddenly Mom began to scream. We all ran into the kitchen thinking she had burned herself, but instead we found her standing next to the ironing board staring straight ahead screaming as loud as she could. I stood there too afraid to move. She was just screaming as if she was trying to get rid of something and the screaming would make it go away.

Life was never the same after that. In the afternoons I came home from school to either an empty house or a quiet one with Mom in bed and the shades drawn. She quit going to church regularly. She left for weeks at a time to different places in the country where she was supposed to get help for her headaches, her depression, *her outbursts*. Every now and then she would surface. Dinnertime would be like the old days. She and Dad would have friends over for Christmas day breakfast. Our birthdays would be celebrated, but we couldn't always count on that.

We never knew what to expect so we learned to tip toe and not do anything to upset her. But she'd eventually get upset about something, usually to do with Dad, and then she'd go to bed for days and we'd all make do without her. I had mixed emotions about her absences. Some days I wanted to stand at the door of her darkened bedroom and yell, "Get out of that damn bed!" *I need you!* Little by little, however, I began to look forward to her days in bed because at least there was peace in our home. Since Mom was acting out, it left no space for me to get into much trouble. I had to be the adult, *which I wasn't good at because I wasn't one,* and gradually my resentment grew.

Not only did we have to tip toe at home, I had to make excuses for Mom's absence at church, and any place else I went alone. I mastered the art of deflection at an early age. No way was I going to tell some nosey, busybody who asked me how my mom was that she had taken too many sleeping pills the night before and she would probably sleep for days. Or that she and Dad were not speaking to each other and her way of getting back at him was to skip church, leaving her spot on the front row conspicuously vacant. Andy and I tried to play counselor at times and earnestly tried to work out the problems between Mom and Dad. It was always to no avail. *Besides, at 13 and 16, what did we know?* What I realize now is that Mom was not going to let anyone work it out. She was depressed and depression was more appealing than waking up to reality and dealing with her problems. She'd rather blame Dad for everything and make him the excuse for all those sedatives she hid and took when no one was looking.

By the time I graduated from college Mom had made three suicide attempts and almost succeeded. Her last attempt was particularly embarrassing because she went to sleep on the Friday night before the Saturday that she and Dad were supposed to host a brunch for more than fifty guests from out of town. I had come home from school to help. Dad woke me up early and said, "Beck, come quick." We could not get Mom to wake up no matter what we did. Dad called an ambulance. The emergency team arrived and rolled Mom out on a stretcher just as the guests were parking their cars and walking up our driveway. The ambulance sped away with the sirens blaring.

It was typical Mom to drown out the brunch people who had come to meet Dad. As I watched it disappear, I felt numb. I should have been worried about Mom. I should have cared more. But I was tired of picking up the pieces of Mom's "cries for help" as one counselor described it. I didn't know if Mom wanted help or not, but surely there was another way to get it. Causing scene after scene only made me angrier and I could not imagine what it was doing to Dad. As a selfish teenager, I didn't try very often. I was a little mad at him too for not "fixing" mom. *After all, he seemed to have the answer to everyone else's problems. Why couldn't he fix theirs?* I didn't understand addiction or depression back then. I didn't know that most addicts are miserable and wished they weren't addicted. My impatience with Mom and lack of compassion for her self-destructive behavior set me up for failure when I married an addict and gave birth to one too.

James was an enthusiastic new Christian when we met. After a short courtship we married planning to live happily ever after. Five years into our marriage he began to drink heavily while the unresolved issues of his past haunted him. He chose alcohol over getting help and our marriage ended the night he came home and picked a fight with my son.

Sarah, who butted heads with James all through high school, reached out for help during her sophomore year of college. After two rehab facilities she came home. For months I lived in the crossfires of the constant clashes between her and her father, which drove her into the arms of a young man she had met in rehab. Suddenly they were pregnant, and our family was in a crisis on top of a crisis. The counselor James and I were seeing advised us to let them decide if they wanted to get married. Sarah was not even 21 yet. No one thought it was a good idea. However, at six months pregnant she walked down the aisle. I spent the year I was getting divorced becoming a new grandmother too. By the time I *was* divorced another baby was on the way. After one year of marriage my new son-in-law abandoned his young family and quickly became my ex-son-in-law. To this day he has not met his second son.

Five years prior to all of that, the counselor I was seeing advised me to go to Al-Anon. Supposedly, they were the relatives of the Alcoholics Anonymous group who met down the hall at the same time Al-Anon met. I didn't want to go. I didn't want to be one of *them*. Even though our marriage was in a free fall and I anticipated lots of counseling in my kids' futures, I was still in the denial phase. Crazy, I know. *Going to Al-Anon showed me just how crazy.*

The first time I went I felt awkward, and I hoped I didn't see anyone I knew. I purposely sat in the back so I could watch and listen through skeptical lenses. The first thing I noticed was the wide socio-economic breadth of the people sitting next to each other. Addiction infected everybody. Evidently it didn't matter if you had loads of money or none at all. "Money can't buy me love," played through my head, *and it can't buy sanity either, nor peace.* The room was packed! The leader welcomed everyone and asked if it was anyone's first time attending. I reluctantly raised my hand. It was obvious I was a newcomer, I could tell by the easy banter among the "regulars" before the meeting started. Someone handed me a "welcome packet" and told me to keep coming back. *I wasn't making any promises.*

The longer I sat there, however, it dawned on me that I must feel how some people feel the first time they go to church, or go back to church, after a long absence. I would tell them to give it a chance and come back. So, maybe I would give these meetings more than one try too. I was familiar with AA, only because my counselor made me read the Big Book. I didn't know there was an equivalent until she made it a homework assignment to attend. I went to the noon meeting because I was afraid to tell my husband that I was going to give it a try. *Wish me luck! I'm going to Al-Anon so I can recover from my addiction to fixing your addiction.*

By the middle of my first meeting I was in tears. I went six times before I said anything. Every time I went, I sat in the back and wept. I could not believe there were so many people who felt the same way I did, who lived with similar circumstances as I did, and who could actually talk about it out loud, *like I couldn't.* I had handled James' addiction like I had handled Mom's- deflection and excuse making. I didn't talk about it. I told myself that I wanted to give him a chance to change without the stigma of people thinking he was broken in some way. Now I realize I was just too proud to admit that we had a problem beyond our control and that we needed more than just a marriage counselor. Unfortunately, he didn't agree. They say that addiction is a progressive disease. There's no taming it, it just gets worse until you kill it, or it kills you. It was killing our marriage, *and it almost killed me.*

Years earlier in our marriage, on a Sunday afternoon, James and I were on our way home from church. We lived near the Chattahoochee River in Atlanta and had to cross a bridge to and from our house every day. That particular Sunday we noticed several people standing on the bridge looking over into the water. We stopped and got out and walked over to see what they were looking at. The police and other kinds of responders were on the bank of the river pulling something out. It was a body. Someone had been killed and thrown into the river upstream months earlier and the body had rotted and decayed as it made its way down to our bridge. I had to turn away as the body got closer to the shore. It was an awful sight. I could not imagine it ever having the soft pink flesh of a human being.

Shortly after Martha's call telling me I had a bitter root judgment against mom, I thought about that day and I realized that resentment is much like that rotting dead body. If not handled properly, it remains at the bottom of our river and moves with the current of our lives. It doesn't stay the same, however, it gets uglier until we finally haul it out and deal with it.

For me, forgiveness had two parts: James' behavior toward me, and my anger at him. I knew I had to own my anger in order to make progress with forgiving him. More so, I knew that if I didn't forgive him I would tether myself to him for the rest of my life, regardless of a piece of paper saying we were no longer man and wife. I pictured carrying around that stinking, rotted dead body of anger and bitterness that no one would want to get near. I knew what I had to do. *I needed courage.*

Though I desperately wanted to be rid of my anger, I secretly dreaded what it might require of me. *"Follow me closely," God had said. But I had not counted the cost.* It seemed like everything I had been taught was put to the test and found wanting. But the truth is, *I* was found wanting. The saying, "It is not what happens to you, but it's how you respond," weighed heavily.

Dealing with my side of the street, as Al-Anon calls it, made me nervous. My Al-Anon sponsor who was a few years ahead of me in her divorce recovery would say, "Becky, give yourself a year, you'll be a different person." *Hello, Becky, meet Becky.* I couldn't imagine life without tight shoulders and a churning stomach. I couldn't imagine having space in my brain for something besides keeping track of the ongoing list of offenses against me and my children. I was tired of trying to anticipate what might happen next, so I could possibly prevent it. I tossed and turned every night justifying my side, pointing my finger, holding all my reasons for resentment close to the chest like a bag of gold, *or thirty pieces of silver.* Jesus was only asking me to do what he did, to forgive as he forgave. *Why was it so hard?*

A friend of mine with whom I had shared my struggle sent me another Keller sermon entitled, Forgiveness. *I desperately needed coaching.* Keller said that when we harbor unforgiveness toward another person we unconsciously "separate our offender from the sea of humanity and we separate ourselves from the sea of sinners." He warned that unforgiveness is a root that works its way to your heart and the evil it is will make you into its own image. *A dried up old woman with a perpetual frown on her face came to mind.*

Keller said that forgiveness is a decision. When we are wronged an emotional debt transpires and someone has to pay. The currency is pain, either mine or my offender's. If I seek vengeance, which always goes beyond justice, I become twisted and evil wins. If I pay it by absorbing the pain myself and I seek the good of the other person, then my anger dissipates because I am no longer feeding it with criticism, gossip, or ill intent toward the person. Eventually evil loosens its grip and then I am not only free, but I've followed in Jesus' footsteps. (Tim Keller, Forgiveness) He didn't sugar coat this process. Nor did he in any way diminish the offense. The sin debt I owed was real, the currency Jesus paid cost Him everything. Keller said, "Put your little story into the big story of what Jesus did for you."

I'm ashamed to say it took time for this to sink in, not because I didn't believe Keller, but because I was blind to the real nature of my sin. I gave theological assent to *being* a sinner, but I did not share the conviction of sin like the tax collector or the woman caught in adultery. Getting divorced finally got my attention. I was a failure and I had contributed to the failure. What was true of everyone else was true of me, I was guilty of going my own way, thinking I knew what was best, fitting God into my plans, full of myself and self-justifying, self-important thoughts. I belonged in the sea of sinners, and if I had any doubts, all I had to do was read my journal entries, listen to my phone conversations, and broadcast my thoughts each time I was with my children during the year and two months it took to finalize everything.

"Therefore, I will give him the honors of one who is mighty and great because he has poured out his soul unto death. *He was counted as a sinner,* and he bore the sins of many, and he pled with God for sinners." (Isaiah 53:12 my italics)

When I read that verse it changed everything I ever thought about forgiveness. If Jesus was willing to stand and be counted as one of us, then

I could do no less and be counted along with my family, *all of them.*

In my prayers I began to picture myself standing shoulder to shoulder next to everyone in my family at the foot of the cross. I confessed *our* sin and I prayed for *our* forgiveness. This helped me more than anything to get to the place where I was ready to forgive.

One night I was driving home feeling lonely and anxious. It sounds crazy but forgiveness felt like I was leaving an old friend behind. My anger and score keeping had been with me so long, I worried about what would take its place? I wanted to be free, *I wanted peace,* but free for what? The gap between God and me had only budged a few inches. I still held Him at a distance for what happened years ago. Though I was making progress, my heart was held hostage by the anger I clung to and yet longed to be freed from. Working through the prayer to forgive felt like I was about to walk the plank. *Would there be anyone to catch me or would I fall into oblivion?* I rarely listened to the radio, *I had temporarily fallen out of love with music, it was too happy, and for a while I was offended by happiness.* But the valet who parked my car that night, must have turned it on and this song was playing, "Never once did we ever walk alone." In disbelief and yet believing God would use even the radio to speak to me, I cried all of the way home. I knew it was God reminding me that regardless of how distant from Him I felt, He had not gone anywhere. He would not wait for me at the end of the plank, He would walk it with me. *Follow Me.*

His presence came in the form of friends like Martha who kept on at me about the prayer. Like my new neighbors who got to know me in spite of myself. And my close friends who didn't abandon me when I took up most of our visits talking about the divorce, the condition of my children, and how hurt and angry I felt.

Finally, I was ready to "work" the prayer about bitter root judgments, and I started with Mom. First, I confessed the list of offenses I was guilty of. I spent time alone in prayer, reading the Bible, and asking God to show me how I had offended Mom and how I had made her feel. When the time came, my heart was ready to own my part. Since she was no longer here, I told God everything I needed to confess. *I begged Him to please pass it along to her if He could. I was really sorry, and I wanted her to know.*

I realized now that forgiveness doesn't mean the wrong didn't really occur or the wrong wasn't really all that wrong. I know this is true because my selfish attitude and lack of compassion toward Mom had been very real. And I wept bitter tears wishing I could tell her in person.

Then I prayed through the list that I needed to forgive her for. After confessing my offenses, hers seemed miniscule. I know they were as real as mine, but now that my heart toward her had changed, I found it easy to forgive her. I actually missed Mom, and I mourned the parts of my childhood I had without her. I wished I could have it back with her in it. All I could do was find comfort in the knowledge that she was with God now, and that she was perfect, happy, and whole.

At the end of the prayer you are supposed to ask God to show you the fruit of your labor, some proof that the work you've done is real and transformative. So I asked, even though Mom was gone. I figured the bigger miracle had already occurred. I had no idea what to expect.

That year two things happened that assured me my prayers had been effective. The first took place as the "fruit" began to blossom in my relationship with Sarah. We'd had a tumultuous ten years, and though I had been her lifeline I had also been her punching bag and her dumping ground. Praying through my anger at Mom had revealed my anger at Sarah. There were similarities between them and I had not always handled things well. The prayer helped me sort through both sets of emotions and in the process I confessed my attitude toward Sarah too. I was determined to make things right with her. Getting it wrong with any of my children was not an option. I would do whatever it took, *God's way though, not mine.*

As a result, the landscape of our relationship began to change, slowly, but surely. The angst I felt every time I was going to be with her melted away. We laughed more. I no longer took personally the parts of her that lashed out because she was dealing with her own set of difficult circumstances.

The second fruit of my prayer began at Mom's funeral and blossomed one weekend when Mom's oldest sister, Aunt Elizabeth, and her daughter, Susan, came to visit me. For years Mom had been estranged from both of her sisters so I rarely saw them, and when I did it was brief and not very personal. At 88, Aunt Elizabeth still worked in her garden, kept the books for her son's business, went to exercise class, and volunteered with other women to make sure that no child in her school district went hungry on the weekends. She was so different from Mom and their younger sister that no wonder it had been hard for the three of them to remain close over the years. But Aunt Elizabeth and I connected immediately! I found that we were fundamentally the same person and I felt a bond with her that I had longed for with Mom and never had. Having Aunt Elizabeth in my life has healed my heart in ways I can't explain. All I know is that I found the female in our family who I take after, look up to and want to emulate. Call it strange, but there is something powerful about that.

Forgiving Mom brought not only peace, but a lighthearted joy I had not experienced since childhood. There were days when my soul swelled with uninhibited love for God and those around me. *Was this happiness?* My heart felt inexplicably full, and I wanted to stay in this space for as long as possible. But there was more work to be done.

I always thought the one thing I would not be able to forgive in a relationship was an affair. No way. That would end my marriage on the spot. But that's not what brought my marriage to an end. It was another one of those things I never saw coming. The night that started the worst year of my life began with an argument and ended with nerve damage to my elbow. Two days later I found myself sitting in the domestic violence office downtown. *I've fallen into someone else's life.* After sitting in line for over an hour, I found myself listening to a girl in her twenties tell me that I did not fill out the report correctly at the doctor's office and my request for a restraining order was denied. *You've got to be kidding! I majored in journalism. I know how to report a story!*

Consequently, I filed for divorce to get the order, which said James could not come within ten feet of me. I didn't believe he would adhere to that rule and I was scared to death for months that he would show up at my door. To make it official, I had to appear before a judge to ask for the order and I brought my police photos with me. After reviewing my folder she looked down at me and said, "Hun, you better get yourself out of this (marriage). Because the next time it will be the hospital, and the next time you'll be dead." I was shocked that she addressed me from her perch on the bench, much less showed any concern. Her words stayed with me throughout that year.

Even though I was praying for a miracle, another thought kept interrupting, *could this be an open door I'm meant to walk through?*

When our marriage began to unravel, I went to see the counselor who encouraged me to go to Al-Anon. She asked me one day, "Becky, who is walking through this with you?" My answer was, "You are." She shook her head and informed me that I needed a lot more support than just hers.

Reluctantly, I told my two best friends the following week. Talking about our marriage had always been off limits and we had adhered to that for twenty plus years. So when I finally mustered the courage to say the words, it felt like betrayal. I became aware of a lot of shame around our family struggle. I was scared of what might happen. I immediately wanted to take my words back. But I was beginning to accept that I needed the support of my friends. For the first time in my life I risked real vulnerability. *Congratulations, it only took fifty years!* The more vulnerable I was the less frightening it became. The women in my life didn't judge me, they rallied around me. I never felt so loved. *Was Mom behind this?*

Next, I called Dad, and then Andy. They were the hardest phone calls to make. I don't know what I was expecting, *a sermon?* But each of them could not have been more gracious. Literally both of their first words were, "Beck, I'm so sorry, I wish you had felt free to tell me sooner." I don't know why I didn't. Dad had been divorced for years. I guess I didn't want to disappoint him. *I was already so disappointed with myself.* Throughout the year it took to get divorced Dad was my rock. He was the hands and feet, and *patient ears,* of Christ for me day after day, *tear after tear.* On the days I felt most alone in the world, I called Dad and his calm soothing voice would assure me that I could make it another day. I believed him, because I knew he had walked this path before.

About two years before the incident occurred, James and I had been seeing another counselor together. I read the books, I did the homework, but we made little progress. Sometimes we saw him separately, and on one occasion he made this statement to me, "Becky, I want you to enter weakness, live confessionally, and look for Christ." I drove home repeating those words over and over. *What did he mean by "enter weakness?"* The concept was foreign. I was used to managing my own soul. In my mind, being weak ran contrary to being a good Christian. If I had a bad habit, I would discipline it till it was gone. If I sinned, I could confess and be forgiven. Even the wrong attitude could be overcome, with time, *and a call to Martha, she would set me straight.* But this was different.

One day I read Philippians 2:5, "Have the same mindset as Christ Jesus." Jesus became a human, subject to everything our bodies are subject too. Jesus considered Himself a servant. Jesus humbled Himself and obeyed His father even when it led Him to a brutal death. Jesus was the ultimate example of "entering weakness." He didn't have anything to confess of his own doing, but He took on my sin and "lived confessionally" for me so on the day that I confessed my sin and asked Him into my heart I could be forgiven. Entering weakness meant putting to death my agenda, my pride, my self-justifying arguments. Entering weakness required that I live everyday with the attitude of a servant, *not my will, but Yours God.* It meant humbling myself daily and living palms up with empty hands. It meant trusting God enough to allow myself to be misunderstood, *and still love the other person, or at least be kind.* Jesus had done the hard part of entering weakness. All he was asking me to do was to walk in his footsteps. *Follow Me closely.*

Entering weakness enabled me to be more vulnerable. All the effort I put into managing my soul and putting up a front that no longer fit on me began to "fall off," as Dad put it. Though nothing about my circumstances had improved, I found myself in a place mentally, emotionally and spiritually that was as foreign to me as Oz was for Dorothy. *Wonderful but a little frightening too.* Christ was my shepherd, He was in the lead, and anything was possible!

When it came time to work through the prayer to forgive James, I felt like I was standing at the foot of an insurmountable mountain. This was not going to happen overnight.

I journaled, I walked, I prayed, and I listened to all kinds of podcasts as I began to own my attitudes of the heart; the attitudes that drained my compassion, that caused me to judge, and that made it easy to withdraw behind a thick wall of brooding silence. I had not understood the internal struggle of an addict. I had not believed that he was as miserable in his world as I was in mine. Once my heart was broken over my own sin, our marriage, and James' struggle, it was not hard to forgive the offenses I once thought were so unforgivable. For me, forgiveness had become not so much about the wrongs done, but about not offending the heart of Christ.

When I finished working through the prayer, I finally got to the point that I could pray for James' wellbeing. *Seek the good of the other, Keller had said.* I desperately wanted our family back together, though I wasn't sure what I was willing for that to look like. I decided to let God choose. I was willing to *be willing* if we were meant to be together, and that was the best I could do.

In the course of time, James married someone else. I won't lie, it came as a shock. I had held out hope for a different outcome, and I didn't know how much it meant to me until a different outcome was no longer an option. My future stretched before me like a wide open highway that I wasn't sure I was ready to explore. Sadness replaced anger, and with it came a new reality- there's no rushing grief.

5

Surrender

"The meaning of our lives emerges in the surrender of ourselves to an adventure of becoming who we are not yet."

Abba's Child, Brennan Manning, p.153

To settle the divorce we decided to go to a mediator rather than go to court. I later wondered if that was the right decision. The days we met with our attorneys and the mediator were exhausting, expensive, and a big waste of time as far as I was concerned. Nothing was ever settled. I would go home tired and angry at everybody involved, including my own attorney. I couldn't wait for this process to be over. I dreaded checking my emails each morning. I hated answering my attorneys' calls. I felt trapped on a Ferris wheel in a hailstorm and I just wanted to get off, go home and be warm and dry again. One evening after another long, unproductive day with no end in sight, I read these verses in Psalms 77:4-9

"You don't let me sleep. I am too distressed even to pray! I think of the good old days long since ended, when my nights were filled with joyful songs. I search my soul and ponder the difference now. Has the Lord rejected me forever? Will he never again be kind to me? Is his unfailing love gone forever? Have his promises permanently failed? Has God forgotten to be gracious? Has he slammed the door on his compassion?"

At least the Psalmist could empathize! I was beginning to wonder if God was even paying attention. One of the biggest lies we are tempted to believe time and time again is that God is not looking out for us. It's what made Eve eat the apple in the most perfect of circumstances, and it was the same lie I struggled with throughout the year and two months it took to untangle a twenty-six-year union.

In response to those verses, I wrote this question in my journal, "Will life ever be good again?" I was beginning to think that since the Bible teaches divorce is man's way for a marriage to end, not God's way, that He was going to hold it against me for the rest of my life. I already felt the shame of failing in the one relationship God had ordained to last a lifetime. Was He going to bail on me now too? Theologically I knew the answer to that question was no. The Bible is too clear about God's "unfailing love" for His children, and that "nothing" can separate us from it. But every day had become a battle for me to hold on to those words, because failure and shame kept launching their assaults. More and more I identified with the man Job who has a book in the Bible named after him. For forty-two chapters Job has a conversation with God debating God's right to obliterate everything he held dear.

In the end, Job comes to this conclusion: "My ears had heard of you, but now my eyes have seen you. Therefore, I despise myself and repent in dust and ashes." (Job 42:5-6) *Is that where this is headed? I thought I knew You Lord. But now I don't even know me. The divorce exposed a side of me that scares me, and now I've experienced a side of You that scares me more.*

In his book, A Grief Observed, C.S. Lewis wrote, "My idea of God is not a divine idea. It has to be shattered time after time. He shatters it Himself. He is the great iconoclast. Could we not almost say that this shattering is one of the marks of His presence?" (p. 52)

In a following passage Lewis makes a statement that begs a question I knew I must answer honestly: "If you're approaching Him not as the goal but as a road, not as the end but as a means, you're not really approaching Him at all." (p. 54) All this time, had I been approaching God as the means to a good life rather than as life itself? How many times had I said to one of my children or to a friend, "If you are looking for life in anything or anyone but God then you are always going to be disappointed." It was *me* who was guilty of that. And I wasn't even looking to *bad* things, I was looking to good things like the lifelong love of a man, godly children, meaningful work. I told myself I was committed to God's will, but maybe it was only as long as it lined up with mine.

Was God shattering my view of Him in order to expose my motives for following Him? Had I lived under assumptions I didn't know I had? The level of my offense toward God over the destruction He allowed in my family, *as if I had not contributed at all,* not only revealed my motives, but unmasked

71

my misinterpretation of the Christian walk I thought I had mastered the fundamentals of. I would never have claimed perfection or even close, *eek!* But I lived as if the rest of what I needed to learn would fit tidily into a framework which overlooked the moment in the Garden of Gethsemane when Jesus prayed to His Father, "Not My will but Yours be done." (Luke 22:42)

Would life ever be good again? I had lost my taste for that question or its answer. Life became good again for Christ after He rose from the dead. But the initial "good" His followers experienced when they realized He had risen was soon replaced by torture, exile and death. What right did I have to desire more than they got? Whether I felt like it or not, I would put one foot in front of the other, and whatever God wanted to do with me from then on was up to Him. I was just beginning to understand for the first time, this really wasn't my life to live, or my story to write. It's His. I'm just the human being in it.

A month after James got remarried, I signed up for a thirteen week class on Monday nights at our church called, The Redemption Series. It was based on a book by Mike Wilkerson, called, Redemption: Freed by Jesus From the Idols We Worship and the Wounds We Carry. It's the story of The Exodus, in the Bible, how God freed the nation of Israel from slavery in Egypt. Wilkerson says that Israel's story is our story too. It's a story of deliverance, ransom, and renewal.

Wilkerson says that we innately know that something has gone wrong in the world and part of the human experience is to try to make sense of it. He says, "it's not our raw experiences that determine our lives, but the meaning we make of them- the stories we tell and the stories we believe. Out of those stories we live our lives." (Redemption p. 22)

The universal human story is that we are all born slaves to sin-sins we've committed and sins that are the result of sin against us- and that's what's wrong in the world. Sin has wreaked havoc on our souls and separated us from the only person who could help us - God. So God sent His son, Jesus, to give His life as a ransom for us. And to each person who believes, God restores that person to his or her original purpose. Wilkerson calls it "renewal" and it's a life-long process. (Redemption p. 37)

It's a process, however, because like Israel, there are some sins we are not ready to let go of. Sometimes our hearts still long for Egypt, for the enslavement of the sins we tell ourselves we enjoy despite the self-destruction they inflict. Once we believe, God patiently but deliberately leads us on the path of restoration to our new life. Our hearts become re-oriented to love God more than we love our sin. We find that peace is preferable to conflict. Love is preferable to hatred. Forgiveness is a lighter load to carry than bitterness.

Working through the prayer to forgive had provided a reboot on that path of restoration, and my once heavy heart was beginning to feel less despondent. But I was barely out of the gate of recovering from twenty-six years of a life I thought would last until "death do us part," when my husband married someone else. I straight up prayed, "Lord, please don't let this sadness last." *I was tired of fake smiles and the phrase, "I'm fine," when I wasn't.*

The first night I sat down at a table next to a young woman named Caroline who I had met before. She was dating one of my best friend's sons, or so I thought. After the general meeting we all divided up into small groups and that was to be our "family" for the next 12 weeks. Caroline and I were not in the same group, but we planned to meet up after and walk to our cars together. When I met up with Caroline she told me that Brett had broken up with her and I could tell in her eyes she was heartbroken, no, heart sick. I knew that look. I saw it in the mirror every day. We immediately bonded and we became allies in our desire to heal, grow and learn from what God had allowed to happen to us.

I devoured The Redemption book. I was hurting, and I was in search of anything to make sense of my pain and to be relieved from it.

"At an emotional level we sense that he (God) is the very source of our pain; it just hurts too much to draw closer to the one who could stop evil but hasn't. So we keep a safe distance. We may hold onto orthodox ideas about Him, but our hearts disconnect; our affection cools; we just don't trust Him. Even here, Jesus knows how you feel. In the garden of Gethsemane he was 'overwhelmed with sorrow, to the point of death.' (Matt. 26:38 NIV). Yet it was in this moment that Jesus addressed the Father in prayer, not with cool formality, but with the familial term of endearment, 'Abba, Father' (Mark 14:36 NIV)." (Redemption p. 52) Wilkerson had just described the condition of my heart more accurately than I could have ever expressed it.

As an adult I trusted God with *almost* all my heart, but I didn't put the full weight of my life on Him, just in case He let me down, like He had Mom and Dad. Now, the cycle of another broken family, with me in it, had repeated itself, unearthing my old wound that time alone could not heal. Was God punishing me? It felt like it. Though, theologically I knew that wasn't true. I knew Christ took my punishment on the cross, and if there was any misunderstanding, it was on my part not His.

Week after week Caroline and I sat together in the large meeting first and went our separate ways to meet with our small group afterward. The class was similar to Al-Anon, and I found this refreshing. We were actually sitting in a church discussing real problems, not just acceptable ones.

The first week we were asked to sign a non-disclosure form so each of us could share without fear of being exposed. Some of the women in my small group would later share appalling stories about their childhoods or marriages. They made my reason for joining seem tame in comparison. But we were told not to compare.

Our first assignment was to write a ten-minute story explaining why we signed up for the Redemption Series. In other words, what happened and why are you here?

The first time I sat down to write, I ended up watching a movie instead. I normally wasn't a procrastinator but something about the assignment made me uncomfortable. The second time, I had the T.V. on and jotted down notes during the commercials. When I looked at them later, I threw them in the trash. What was wrong with me? Why was I avoiding this simple exercise? Finally, one Saturday morning, *it was due that Monday night,* I sat with my computer on and the T.V. off and asked God for *real* help this time. As understanding dawned, I typed as fast as I could. *Was this really my story?*

Along with the Redemption book, I had been reading a book by Don Miller called, Scary Close, and it was the story of his journey to relational health and authenticity. In it he is transparently honest as he sorts through the "scary" truth of how we often choose the kind of person we end up with: "On a subconscious level we are drawn to the negative characteristics of our primary caretakers." If we perceive that we didn't have the love and approval of someone like our mom or dad when we were young, then we perceived that our basic needs like "food, shelter and love were under threat." (Scary Close p.209-210) Later in life when we meet someone who exhibits their negative qualities "our brains become attached to this random person thinking if we could just fix some of those negative qualities in ourselves we could have security and never worry about food, shelter, or love again." (Scary Close p. 210)

We mistake attraction, in whatever form, for what is actually a deep need to heal our own wounds. Our strong desire to take care of "unfinished business" in our relationship with that initial caretaker trumps all else and the initial passion we feel ends up being a bomb that explodes in our face. (Scary Close p.210) I was vaguely familiar with this concept before reading Don's book, but I preferred to ignore it because of its implications. However, Don's courage to admit this repetitive dynamic in his life, gave me the courage to look at it again.

Had I subconsciously chosen James in order to achieve some kind of healing from my relationship with Mom? Had something inside me needed to recover love and acceptance so badly from her that I attempted to fix myself by gaining it from someone who was less capable of providing it than she was? What drove me to make such a decision? I wouldn't have the answer for at least another two years.

God was using my broken heart to crack open a part of my soul that I was completely unfamiliar with and wasn't sure I even *wanted* to explore. "Which is more painful?", I read one morning, "To live without hope or to catch a glimpse of hope, only to have it disappear? Often, this is our experience on the eve of redemption. Certainly, God is not a fickle redeemer. He is faithful. But if we expect redemption to be mainly about comfort, we may be disappointed when – at least for a season- it brings more pain." (Redemption p. 56) *And self-loathing, embarrassment and OMW, is that really who I am?*

My ten-minute story would be the debut of the most humiliating self-discovery I had ever made- *"I was raised by my mom and I married my mom."* My discomfort level rose, while my excitement over the class diminished. However, I wasn't a quitter, *being divorced compelled me to prove this to an imaginary critic somewhere,* so for that reason alone I wrote the most honest confession I had ever admitted, even to my own journal. "My childhood and young adulthood were characterized by living on high alert..." I timed it twice to make sure I didn't go past the ten-minute mark.

That Monday I was determined to read mine first so I could get it over with. I was shaking. Not even five years in Al-anon had prepared me to be this vulnerable in front of a group. When I finished, my heart was pounding, I thought I might faint, but instead I reached for the tissue box that sat in the middle of our circle. I needed a distraction so I didn't have to look at anyone in the eye.

After each "share" we were allowed to ask questions or make affirming comments, but we were not allowed to try to fix the other person's problems. I still had my guard up so this came as a relief. I was *not* ready to invite anyone in past the foyer of my soul, especially now that I was aware of spaces I had not yet inspected. *I'll clean out my own closets thank you very much.* The comments from the group were kind and tentative. *We were all new at this.* I thanked each person and breathed a sigh of relief.

Monday nights came and went and I realized that God was healing my wounds without me. I was no longer meddling in my spiritual journey like I had done for years, thinking it was up to me to improve myself by telling the stories that fit my narrative. He was in charge now. But I was uncomfortable about identifying my idols. What *was* an idol? *I thought they only existed in the Bible and old movies.*

Wilkerson quoted Tim Keller who summed up idols as, "Anything more important to you than God...Anything that becomes more fundamental than God to your happiness, meaning in life and identity." For examples of idols, Keller lists, "love, sex, money, power, success or religion." (Redemption p. 123) The more I read the book and the more our small group discussed idols, I came to understand them as more relevant replacements of God like, the approval of others, material possessions, beauty, food, even family. None of these are bad things in themselves. The deceit comes in when we commit ourselves to an idol rather than to God. We love it and we nurture it and we believe that it is doing for us what only God can do. But Idols don't fill the hole in our hearts, they don't solve our problems, and they can't free us from addictions we *want* to quit.

I soon discovered what was in my closets that I didn't want anyone to see. I had shelves of idols I kept for emergencies when it seemed like God was not going to answer a prayer the way I thought he should. My idols were good things, for the most part, like family, high performance in my role as a wife and mom, beauty, approval, and good food. There was also a box of perfectionism, but knowing I had inherited that box from mom, I was aware of the dangers of bringing it out too often. Though it didn't always stop me. These were the idols I clung to and, yes, worshipped without knowing it. I had Christ, and I had these, and together they made up my value and my self-worth.

Idols obstruct our relationship with God in a way that can deceive us, especially someone like me. The problem is when good things become idols they turn into a "sinful desire masquerading as an innocent need." (Redemption p.109) They don't stay in the closet either. They might take turns being center stage, but eventually they replace God, and *He* is the one who gets taken in and out of the closet instead. We begin to think of our idols as rights. We deserve them and we want

God to approve of them and even *improve* them. Just like the Israelites did.

I had gone a long time thinking that my interpretation of life, my story, was the correct one. I was blind to the dynamic going on between God and me. The distance I had kept Him at had not stayed the same. The gap between God and me widened as life got more complicated and I leaned on my idols more than I leaned on Him. Like any good parent He had to do something, otherwise I would self-destruct. Actually, He didn't have to do anything. I experienced the most powerful life changing correction a child can have- *the natural consequences of my behavior.* Just like in life, a marriage that is no longer centered on God, the one who created it, will not stand the test of time, or teenage children, or a new business or an addiction.

Not one single idol was allowed in the Israelites' tents without it enraging God and leaving several deaths in his wake. (Joshua 7) That seemed harsh when I read it as a teenager, but reading it now with a broken heart that was searching for answers, I was mortified that I had committed the same offense against a holy God who had loved me with the life-long love I had always wanted from a man and now mourned that I no longer had.

Even though I deserved it, God did not hold against me the distance I kept Him at for most of my life, nor the idols, *not just one,* that I clung too instead of Him. Two thousand years ago, Jesus had a choice, and He chose the cross in spite of my dishonesty about my sin, disloyalty in the face of His sacrifice, and resentment because He didn't answer a childhood prayer the way I thought He should. I was guilty, but *not* charged, because instead of giving me what I deserved, He took my punishment for me, and then He invited me to join Him on a life-long walk, *even He knows my love language,* offering His constant companionship of: love not selfishness, peace with no drama, patience that is never exhausted, kindness with no strings attached, goodness you can count on, gentleness instead of sarcasm, self-control in every circumstance, and a hilarious sense of humor. Who doesn't want a man who loves like that?

For me, getting my priorities back in line with God's priorities involved surrender. I was ready to give up my disappointment with Him and put Him front and center where He belonged. One day I pictured us sitting across the kitchen table from each other. *Any conversation that mattered always happened at the kitchen table when I was growing up.* I had cleaned out my closets, and all my possessions, including the love of my children, and what other people think, my future, *everything,* was laid out between us. I looked at Him straight in the eyes and I shoved it all over to His side of the table. And I said, "Lord, take it all, and only give me back what You want me to have. But don't give me anything that will ever threaten our relationship again." Through forgiveness

I had learned to trust. And through trust I was learning to receive God's love and love Him back.

At the end of the Redemption book, Wilkerson warns the reader against two things: The first, is using God to fix what we don't like about ourselves. "Here, near the end of a book that you probably picked up because you were seeking transformation and freedom, it may be hard to swallow the idea that such goals could be hollow. But here's the catch: they are only hollow when they are not filled with God." "In other words, we don't just get peace from God; God *is* our peace. He gives us himself." (Redemption p. 161) The same is true for love, hope, and joy. God's presence is where real transformation takes place. He says, "it isn't that we should stop wanting freedom from addiction, healing for the wounds of our past, or repair for our broken relationships today. It is that those blessings all come to us in God's presence and lead us further into his presence. He is the greatest gift he gives." (Redemption p. 162)

The second warning is that "the Christian who is content with the presence of sin should not be surprised to feel the absence of God's peace." (Redemption p.168) We have to "declare war" on anything that separates us from God. But He does not expect us to go into battle alone. He helps us, all we have to do is ask.

In the end, God drives out the enemies for the Israelites, and they finally make it to their destination. "This is the land they have longed for all their lives, the land they'd spoken of from generation to generation throughout their entire captivity in Egypt and their journey through the wilderness...they were finally home." (Redemption p. 170)

About two months into the class, I left my ear buds at home to go for a walk. I no longer needed another voice as a distraction. The sadness I felt at the beginning of the class had begun to fade. It was no longer my dominant emotion. I remembered reading this sentence by Verdell Davis who had lost her husband unexpectedly in a plane crash: "Somewhere along the way, letting him go became a *choice* I had to make." (Riches Stored in Secret Places, Verdell Davis p.109) I knew I needed to make that choice too. Subconsciously I had confused letting go of a person with letting go of a life I would no longer have. To be certain, losing James *did* mean losing a familiar way of life, but it didn't mean that another kind of existence couldn't unfold or be just as fulfilling, *and perhaps more.* One day I read, "This is what the Lord says, 'Stop at the crossroads and look around. Ask for the old, godly way, and walk in it. Travel its path, and you will find rest for your souls.' But you reply, 'No, that's not the road we want'." (Jeremiah 6:16)

I admit it, I didn't want to have to choose at all. I wanted to stay married, raise grandchildren together, plan trips together, and grow old together. I wanted the problems to go away, and I wanted my original choices to stay intact. But I was at a crossroads whether I liked it or not. As much as I had loved my husband and loved many things about our life together, I *had* to let go of him. One day I was on a walk thinking about the crossroads that lay ahead, I had no idea what "the old, godly way" would look like for me, but I desperately wanted "rest" for my soul. So I stopped where I was, threw up my hands and told God, "Lord, you gave him to me once, now I give him back to you." And that was it.

On the last night of the Redemption class we held a celebration where everyone brought food, and whoever wanted to, was free to get up and share what they had learned. I wasn't much braver, but I was willing to be more vulnerable, so I decided to write something and share it with the large group. It could only last two minutes.

I talked about the idols I had identified and given up to God, and I thanked everyone who taught for being so open about theirs. Again, my heart was pounding as I spoke, but I was so grateful for the courage I was given to do it. I conquered something on the inside that night, I should say God did it for me. All I know is that for the first time, I felt less afraid of admitting who I might *not* be, and more comfortable with telling who I actually am.

Afterward, while everyone was eating, a woman came up to me and thanked me for sharing. She said she struggled with the same idols and hearing me confess mine, gave her the courage to deal with hers too. *God always has an agenda bigger than the one we think it is, and it usually involves sharing what we have been given.*

My friend Caroline made a lot of progress throughout the course as well. She had dealt with some hard family relationships as well as her broken heart. Brett was in God's hands, and in the meantime she decided to go back to school for another degree.

Not only did that end up being a great career decision for her, but it also got Brett's attention and he began to pursue her again. Three years later he proposed and now they are married.

Reconciliation occurred for me too. The distance between God and me had begun to close. Now, I couldn't imagine "us" any other way. He had never stopped pursuing me. I named it, "the magnetic love of Jesus." There is no such thing as flying under God's radar, and now I ask, *who would want too?*

One day I read, "We can make our plans, but the Lord determines our steps." (Prov. 16:9 NLT) I felt God take my cheeks in both of His hands and turn my head in a new direction. *"Becky," He whispered, "It's time to stop looking back."* I had no idea where His steps would take me, but it no longer mattered. I had locked arms with Christ, and for the first time in a long while, I no longer feared what might lay ahead.

6

The Snag

"Joy sometimes needs pain to give it birth."

Streams in the Desert, p. 352

For a long time I thought of divorce and the aftermath like a long tumble down a high mountain. When I finally landed at the foot of the mountain, it took a while to get my bearings. I had twigs in my hair, some dirt in my mouth and a few scrapes that would need tending, but for the most part I survived. Now I had to get up and walk again.

One day I read this sentence in a book about recovery, "No one heals in a straight line." (The Choice: Embrace the Possible, p. 157) The author, Edith Eger, was an Auschwitz survivor. If anyone deserved to zig-zag, she did. In the story of her journey back to emotional healing and wholeness she is refreshingly transparent about her struggles and insecurities as well as her own marriage. Even though my experience was nothing like hers, her story gave me the permission I needed to be human, mistakes and all, while I learned how to walk again as a single woman. I *so* related to Jerry Sittser's lament when he wrote, "My quest for a new identity seems repulsive to me. Do I really want the kind of life I now have?" (A Grace Disguised: How the Soul Grows Through Loss p. 84) *No I don't!* The last thing I wanted to be at fifty-two was single. Awkward, unsure of myself, and suddenly too shy to speak to my friends' husbands, were my new normal. The naked finger on my left hand felt like a billboard advertising the biggest failure of my life.

As I put one foot in front of the other every day, I began to accept acceptance and reject denial. One day I read, "Loss forces us to see the dominant role our environment plays in determining our happiness...it exposes the true state of our soul. Finally, we reach the point where we begin to search for a new life, one that depends less on circumstances and more on the depth of our souls." (A Grace Disguised: How the Soul Grows Through Loss p. 89) *It's taking longer than I thought it would, Lord.*

By the time I was six years out from the divorce, I was doing okay, not great, at least that's how I described it to myself. I had started a new career, I had as good of a relationship as I could with each of my children, I led a small group of women that met together after the redemption class was over, and I had the best women friends I had *ever* had. Even so, I was still occasionally "ambushed by grief", a term I learned in the one and only Divorce Care class I went to shortly after our divorce ended.

At the urging of a well-meaning friend I reluctantly attended the class that met at my church one Wednesday evening. *I had a minus ten desire to go, but I went anyway.* After introducing ourselves to each other, they showed a short video about divorce. During the film I was struck at how universal the fallout of a broken marriage is. One phrase in particular stood out. The narrator said don't be surprised if in the course of your day you hear a song, or have a memory and suddenly you are overwhelmed with sorrow. This is called being "ambushed by grief." I immediately adopted that phrase and it became a life raft for me when I was reminded of a happy moment in my marriage which made our divorce and the reasons behind it all the more sad. I would remind myself that the tears running down my cheeks were normal and that they would soon pass. I learned not to fight the sorrow, but to breath it in and then let it go.

Still, I felt like there was a part of me that was caught on a brier like the ones I grew up with in my back yard. Once that sharp thorn got a hold of you, it was hard to get free. I continued to read in search of the one answer, that missing piece of my puzzle, that would pull everything together for me. I listened to more podcasts, I made it a point to ask other people how they got over their divorce, but I just couldn't seem to put a name to what was bothering me. Some days I lived on the verge of tears without a specific reason. I no longer grieved the loss of my marriage. I was beginning to like my new life. I had moments of happiness, but no lasting joy. *Surely this wasn't going to be my version of "As Good as it Gets?"*

The book I read by Don Miller, called Scary Close, tells how he went to a place called On Site in Nashville, Tennessee. It was like adult camp for people who had experienced grief and loss, family dysfunction, emotional trauma, divorce. He was refreshingly honest about how the therapists enabled him to unravel some of his childhood memories and how his relationship with little Don had affected decisions made by big Don. Think the movie, The Kid. The conversations he described with the people at On Site made me yearn to go. I had never thought about my childhood the way the therapists at On Site portrayed it. What *did* I think of little Becky? My brother found her annoying. Did I?

I recommended Scary Close to everyone I knew and even gave several copies away. My daughter and son read it and for a while we talked about Don and Don's fiancé, Betsy, as if they were close friends. I think I kept hoping that Don's awakening and Betsy's relational health would rub off on me and I would catch whatever they had. But a year later, I had not made much progress, I was stuck and desperately wanted to get unstuck. So one spring day I called On Site and asked if they had a spot for me in June. I literally went the week of my birthday. *Surprise!*

The first session was on trauma and the brain. I wrote furiously even though I was not sure this subject applied to me. The speaker explained that while we attribute trauma to soldiers in times of war, we diminish our own trauma, and live in denial about it. This helps us survive. We make excuses for it, and we might even convince ourselves we deserve it.

The speaker went on to define emotional abuse as being active energy toward a child, and emotional neglect as active energy away from a child. Both of these are trauma. Then he made this statement, "When a child is abused by a parent he doesn't stop loving the parent, he stops loving himself." Those words stopped me in my tracks. Though I didn't understand it yet, the speaker had just hit my bull's eye.

One day, a year after I went to On Site, I was walking with a friend from my Redemption group. We were talking about Luke's relationship to James. They had not seen each other in almost a year because James refused to see him. My friend asked me, did your mom ever do that to you? *A voice inside whispered, "pay attention to that question."* As I answered her, "no," I realized that Mom never refused to physically see me, she just never genuinely and sustainably connected with me as a child. Perhaps in my earliest years she tried, but once her depression set in, whatever connection we had was lost.

At On Site they showed us a video of a child's response to his mother's face. When the mother engaged and smiled and cooed the child was happy and responsive. But then the mother turns her face away and when she faces the child again, she remains stoic, unresponsive, disengaged. The child reacts by reaching out to her and trying to get her attention, he makes loud noises, and when that doesn't work, he gets upset and begins to cry. Their point was that when a child loses that connection with a parent and never gets the chance to re-connect, emotional trauma occurs, and the child may develop self-destructive behavior to cope with the lack of connection. The list included substance abuse, self-harm, co-dependency, gambling, eating disorders, and even suicide. The reason for the self-destruction is because of what the speaker said, the child quits loving himself, not the parent.

From my earliest memories of Mom, I didn't feel connected with her. One, because she allowed Virginia to become my temporary emotional connection when she came to visit, and two, because all of our conversations were about her and never me. Regardless of what the subject started out as, it ended up about Mom. Subconsciously I spent much of my life trying to reconnect with Mom and people like Mom. I never felt like I measured up to an imaginary standard that I made up to explain the reason why we weren't connected. My self-destructive behavior took all kinds of forms, but the worst was co-dependency and shame. These were things I found it hard to accept about myself, but once I identified them, their grip on me slowly began to loosen. I was able to identify my unhealthy behavior, and as a result my relationship to myself, to my children and my own family began a gradual shift toward wholeness. All this took time, lots of time.

Though Mom's behavior angered and frustrated me as a young person, I now look back on her with compassion. I believe Mom sincerely sought answers for her depression, I'm just not sure she was ever willing to face the truth about it. I'll never understand, but her example kept me motivated to keep on climbing out of the dark hole of my own grief and loss.

Throughout the week at On Site, I listened, took copious notes, got to know my roommates, *forced myself to talk to strangers,* and took as many walks as possible. All the information was good. I just wasn't sure about the parts that applied to me. The leaders had said that one week at On Site was equal to nine months of therapy. I decided to give myself time and "trust the process" as they put it. In the afternoons I sat on my bed or on a bench outside and reviewed my notes from the morning sessions.

"Vulnerability is the birthplace of joy and creativity," said the speaker one morning. I was becoming more vulnerable, but I still lacked joy and creativity. The feeling that I was on trial to see how I would handle the big life exam I had been given remained, and that shut down joy every time it tried to surface. I still struggled with the shame of my divorce and of being physically hurt. Underneath, I began to suspect that shame had existed before my divorce, and in some ways had contributed to the problems on "my side of the street" in regard to the issues in our marriage that are common to a lot of couples.

On another day the speaker said, "Shame is a soul eating emotion." As children we think, if I'm going to risk losing your (the parent's) love, then

I will suppress my emotions." I had suppressed my emotions for years, first with my own family, then in my marriage, then with my children. But by discounting what I thought and what I felt, I had muzzled the true me.

Now I realized that I could not surrender that which I was not willing to own. I was angry that I wasted so much time *not* being honest, authentic and vulnerable. I hated how I had appeased others at my own expense. What did that say about the kind of relationship I had with them? Even scarier what did it say about my relationship with myself? Perhaps my anger should really be directed at me. *Then I discovered that some of it was.*

One morning the speaker called up a young woman and gave her a heart pillow. He asked her to give it to someone then take it away and give it to someone else and so on. His point was that deep down we sense something's wrong, incomplete, missing. Therefore, we export our self-care expecting others to make us feel special and make up for that nameless void. When they don't fill our cup, because they were never meant to, we take our "heart" back and give it to someone else and we continue to do that because we think it's someone else's job to "complete" us. But no one can complete us. It's our job to address the nameless missing piece and to make peace with it.

On Site believes that process involves making peace with our inner child. One morning the speaker said to ask ourselves, "How would I greet me as a kid?" Would I be happy to see me? Or would I be annoyed or feel like I was being interrupted? What would I say and how would I, the child, respond? Tears swelled up as I hurried to write these sentences down and avoid eye contact with the speaker.

I began to think of my grandsons and how tenderhearted I felt toward them. I had no expectations surrounding them. I expected them to be the exact ages they were including all the mess and commotion that comes with it. Nothing more. I had to admit I had never felt that way about myself. I cut little me no slack in the throes of life. In fact, it was then that I realized I was my biggest critic and worst best friend.

I had dragged little Becky through so much performance-based acceptance, and self-destructive behavior, and guilt trips for not handling life better. One night while I hoped my roommates were asleep, I wept over how I had treated little Becky as I visualized me at my grandson's ages. How could I have been so hard on myself? How could I have expected unprepared me to know how to handle a suicidal mom, my brother's adolescent criticisms, and my parents' volatile marriage? So many mixed messages for a little person to decipher and make sense of. How could I *not* partially blame myself for their behavior? *And yet there I was in my subconscious, the determined survivor, waving the white flag, willing to forgive, crying for help, hoping for love.*

I suddenly realized I had a big job ahead of me. I wasn't sure how to even begin. One day I read this sentence, "Divine forgiveness leads to self-forgiveness." (A Grace Disguised: How the Soul Grows Through Loss p. 104) That was it. I had to forgive myself for being such an *idiot* and learn to love myself. If God forgave me, I could forgive me. There would be things I wish I could go back and undo, but I couldn't. Like the prayer we often prayed in Al-Anon, I would have to learn to "accept the things I cannot change, change the things I can, and have the wisdom to know the difference." (The Big Book of AA)

At fifty-seven I would finally make peace with little me, and I would begin a new journey, but not in survival mode as I had been for years. No more would I play the role of the overly critical, impossible-to-please hall monitor of my own soul. Instead, I would learn to "play at life" again, like our morning speaker encouraged us to do. My love of music would be rekindled, and I would sing more, dance more, laugh more, and rest in two certainties: One, that my heavenly Father loves me and forgives me, *not just because He has to because He's God,* but because He *wants* to, and He has deposited His love inside of me for eternity. And two, that I no longer had to live on high alert because little Becky would be under my fierce protection, and our relationship would be comprised of boundaries, love, trust, and the freedom to use our voice.

All of this took time. In fact, it took a year after I left On Site for me to process what I learned that one week. But over time, the grief that made me feel adrift for so long melted away. The emotional brier that held me back finally broke, and I was free.

7

The Scar

"Whatever happened in the life of Jesus
is in some way going to happen to us.
Wounds are necessary. The soul has to
be wounded as well as the body. To think
that the natural and proper state is to be
without wounds is an illusion. Those who
wear bulletproof vests protecting themselves from failure, shipwreck, and heart-
break will never know what love is. The
unwounded life bears no resemblance to
the Rabbi."

Abba's Child, Brennan Manning, p.158

In March, after mom had died the previous November, I invited Martha to come speak to a group of my friends about the Bitter Root Judgment Prayer. Life was finally settling into a new rhythm, though it would be another year before I had fully worked through the prayer myself. Nonetheless, I was anxious to share what I was learning with others who I knew would be interested and who would benefit from hearing Martha explain it. I reserved the common room in my building and bought lunch for everyone who said they could come. I was nervous and excited about what the response might be. For me, it was another risk in being vulnerable, but oddly the pain I had experienced propelled me forward like a World War II Kamikaze pilot. I had lost what was most precious to me, what else did I have to lose? The friends who came listened with open hearts. Their questions were sincere and their comments were constructive. Some of them committed to work through the prayer for specific relationships in their own lives. Later I received calls and emails from them telling me how working the prayer changed them and their perception of the "problem" person and how that particular relationship was beginning to improve.

The following year I was asked to host the same talk again, and this time I led the discussion by sharing my own story of forgiveness. Though I stumbled, fell, and recovered almost daily, I had started this journey and there was no turning back. I had tasted the freedom that comes with knowing that vulnerability leads to open doors, not closed ones, and that at the end of the day being authentic and true is easier than yanking on and tugging at a façade that keeps slipping because it doesn't fit who I am or who I want to be anymore.

In that same March I realized that my elbow was not going to heal on its own and that it was time for me to do something about it. I had put off surgery as long as I could in order to help Sarah adjust to having a new baby and a toddler. The doctors had advised me to wait a year in case my elbow returned to normal. But instead of healing, it steadily grew worse, so early one morning my friend Laura drove me to the hospital and waited for me while the doctor moved the nerve in my elbow to the side of my arm. Right before I went in to the surgery room, and the drugs were beginning to take effect, I hazily heard Laura lecture the doctor about the scar I would have. She said to him, "Now don't you leave an ugly scar on Becky. She can still wear sundresses and she doesn't need a big scar running down the back of her arm. Do you hear me?" My lights went out before I heard his answer, but she got her point across. When it was all said and done, I only had a dainty scar, not too terribly long, on the back of my right arm. The scar is not what bothered me so much as the limited use of my hand and wrist.

It took over two years to feel somewhat back to normal, though even now my right arm and wrist aren't as strong as my left.

I admit there was a period where I fought resentment every time I iced my arm at the end of a day. The pain was real, the offense was real, and my anger was real. These were the things that Christ came to deal with when He became a man, then a sacrifice, then a King.

In another book by Tim Keller called, Jesus the King, Keller explains the story, as told in the book of Mark, chapter 4, verses 36-41. Jesus and the disciples are in their fishing boat crossing the Sea of Galilee. Jesus had been teaching all day, so He decided to go down below and take a nap. A storm comes and the boat nearly sinks. The frightened disciples awaken Jesus with these words, "Don't you care if we drown?" The storm was severe and even though they were experienced sailors, they thought they were going to die. Jesus gets up and says to the wind and the waves, "Quiet! Be Still!" Keller says, "This picture goes to our hearts, because everyone who's ever tried to live a life of faith in this world has felt like this sometimes. Everything is going wrong, you're sinking, and God seems to be asleep, absent, or unaware. If you loved us, the disciples were saying, you wouldn't let us go through this." (Jesus the King p. 53) *My thoughts exactly.*

"But if Jesus is God, then he's got to be great enough to have some reasons to let you go through things you can't understand...He can love somebody and still let bad things happen to them, because he is God-and because he knows better than they do." (Jesus the King p. 54)

God knew it would take a storm to disrupt my narrative of how life should go. I needed nothing short of the demolition of my soul to change my thinking, reset my priorities, and transform my heart to be able to receive God's love and give God's love away.

Philippians 2:8 says, "And being found in appearance as a man, he humbled himself by becoming obedient to death- even death on a cross."

Jesus willingly suffered the "ultimate storm" for my sake, by going to the cross for my sin, so how can I ever ask the question again, "God, don't You care?" *Don't You care about my marriage? Don't You care about the pain my children are in and the scars they will carry for the rest of their lives? Couldn't You have accomplished Your will another way?*

"And if you know that he did not abandon you in that ultimate storm, what makes you think he would abandon you in the much smaller storms you're experiencing right now?" (Jesus the King p. 57-58) What it took a storm to teach me was, the storms of life are not the issue. The truth of God's overwhelming love for us proved by the death and resurrection of His Son is the issue. And to the degree that I live in humble, confessional, surrendered, obedience to Him, the storms that rise up and try to sink me will no longer matter. Regarding my family, I began to mentally put everyone I cared about in God's hands each morning and literally walk out the door. One day as I was praying for my children, *and fretting over the state of their hearts*, God said, "Give them to Me and go." So I did.

What about my future? What now? Keller answered by telling the reader that the Kingdom of God is coming where all relationships will be healed and where we will experience true Shalom. "And to the extent that that future is real to you, it will change everything about how you live in the present." (Jesus the King p. 222)

As the disciples watched Jesus die, they thought His scars had ruined their lives. But afterward, when Jesus appeared to them and showed them His resurrection body with the scars still there, the sight of those wounds and the memory of them no longer made them sad. Jesus' scars hadn't ruined their lives, they actually saved the disciples' lives. And the memory of Jesus' scars would help them when they were tortured and beaten for carrying the message of his resurrection to the rest of the world. (Jesus the King p. 224)

The night that I was hurt felt like my world came to an abrupt end. I saw nothing good that could come out of it. Looking back, I realize now that God let His purpose mixed with man's sin play out all under his sovereign supervision. I learned that God *will* take us to the edge and even let us fall over it if that's what it takes to bring us into a transformative relationship with Him. My arm won't ever be the same, but neither will my relationship with Christ.

This passage in Keller's book filled me with hope in my darkest moments more than anything else I read during that season of my life: "On the day of the Lord- the day that God makes everything right...you will find that the worst things that have ever happened to you will in the end only enhance your eternal delight. On that day, all of it will be turned inside out and you will know joy beyond the walls of the world. The joy of your glory will be that much greater *for every scar you bear.*" (Jesus the King p. 224-225 my italics)

8

The Climb

"I have told you these things, so that in me
you may have peace. In this world you
will have trouble. But take heart!
I have overcome the world."

John 16:33

By far, the hardest part about the divorce, for me, was the risk of losing the love of my children. We had always been close. But when I was the one who filed for divorce, I was the one everybody blamed for breaking up our family. As a result, my children backed away one by one. A thick wall of anger, resentment, blame *and something that felt like hatred*, divided us and I was not allowed to climb over it and explain my side. I couldn't sleep at night because of the fear that my children would choose their dad over me; that they wouldn't be able to have a relationship with both of us. That he would "win" and I would be exiled to a foreign part of their lives that they no longer wanted to visit.

Each of my children handled the divorce differently, but anger was the common thread. No one dared cross the line with their father, so I found myself on the receiving end of their short fuses. Tempers that I knew were fueled by fear of the future, frustration over circumstances they had no control, and disappointment with the two people in their lives they thought would never let them down this far exploded with regularity. With each angry word and raised voice my fear was reinforced, *they will hold this against me for the rest of my life.* I felt so misunderstood. Children count on the stability parents are supposed to provide. I had destroyed that stability with a signature that had officially disconnected our family. Their anger broke me. This was the fallout I wasn't sure I could survive.

Early during the divorce proceedings, I sought the advice of a few women whom I respected and who I knew had experienced a divorce too. I wanted to know how they handled their relationships with their children most of all. My broken heart could wait, but not theirs. Underneath their brave facades I knew their lives had come crashing down like mine. I desperately wanted to roll back time and be in our kitchen again, sitting on the counters, eating leftovers, telling jokes. Prior to the first holidays after our separation, a friend gave me this advice, she said, "Becky, be the person your children have always known you to be and do what you have always done. If you made turkey and dressing, then make it. If you stuffed the stockings at Christmas, then stuff them. Just be the steady one. That's what they need." Her words anchored me throughout the next several years.

"Be the steady one." Though this was my goal, I didn't always succeed. I worked hard not to notice the change in my children's demeanor toward me. *I missed the familiarity, their smiles, their trust.* I struggled not to take it personally. I had soul crushing interactions with each of them during the years that followed. It was in those moments most of all that I learned what it cost to really love another human being. It took my children's brokenhearted rage and rejection to show me how I had committed the same offense against my heavenly father who with unfailing love and patient forbearance withstood *my* resentment and cold shoulder toward Him most of my life because I disagreed with the story He allowed to play out in my own family. How could I hold my children's behavior against them when God had not held mine against me?

One morning I read, "Therefore, since we are surrounded by such a great cloud of witnesses, let us throw off everything that hinders and the sin that so easily entangles. And let us run with perseverance the race marked out for us, fixing our eyes on Jesus, the pioneer and Perfecter of our faith. For the joy set before him he endured the cross, scorning its shame, and sat down at the right hand of the throne of God. Consider him who endured such opposition from sinners, so that you will not grow weary and lose heart." (Hebrews 12:1-3 NIV)

No one can walk the path that Jesus walked without it costing what it cost him-everything. Loving, serving, and continuing to engage our "enemies," especially when they wear the beloved faces of our own children, required a kind of crucifixion that I was only willing to endure because it was for their sakes, not mine. *God knows where we live.* Is this what it took for the "perfecter of my faith" to bid me to follow Him on "the way of suffering," so that I would learn to love and forgive like He loves and forgives me?

Days, months and years passed as this process played out in my life and in my relationship with each of my children. All I could do was wait and give them room to sort out their own ideas about what had happened to our family and how they felt toward me.

One day I read, "I will give you a new heart and put a new spirit in you; I will remove from you your heart of stone and give you a heart of flesh." (Ezekiel 36:26) During the waiting years with the children, *it felt more like I was holding my breath*, I fasted and prayed on Mondays. I wanted God to take away the stony parts of my heart. I wanted to be ready for what came next in my life. And I make no apologies that part of my motive was the children. *God even though you and I are on better footing, please put it in their hearts to forgive me, to understand, and to love me again.*

Proverbs 17:9 says, "Love prospers when a fault is forgiven, but dwelling on it separates close friends." I desperately wanted love to prosper again in my family and during those days of fasting God enabled me to forgive all the behavior and hurtful words carte blanche. *Wasn't this what His grace looks like toward me?* Fasting didn't earn me any credits with God, *there are no credits to earn, just Jesus,* but I was finally coming to an understanding about the heart of God. In my brokenness God was inviting me into the intimate relationship He had always wanted with me. I could no longer hold Him at arm's length and follow Him closely at the same time.

Long before I was reconciled to my children, I decided to follow God, *His way not mine*, regardless of what I lost in the process. Matthew 16:25 was true, "whoever loses his life for my sake will find it." I had to "lose" the privilege to be close to my children again if I ever hoped to gain their trust back. If I didn't keep Christ front-and-center I would ruin whatever attempts were made by me or them. Like a long hike on a rocky path, the mending began.

At first there were misunderstandings, tears, and division, but then clarity began to dawn. Authenticity replaced fear, something like friendship formed, the love that never disappeared, *it just got buried,* resurfaced, and ultimately the chaos we had lived with for so long was replaced with a tenuous, but recognizable peace we all mutually wanted restored.

Peace, not always harmony, but a willingness to align ourselves with one another became our "new normal." Over time, we figured out how to do holidays differently. Birthdays were celebrated together again. Having the little ones brought more laughter and play back into our lives. We all began to breathe easier as we allowed each other the space to find new footing, and learn to accept the different landscape of our family.

Now I try to be more like my grandsons, I live one day at a time and I don't worry about tomorrow. I now know I have a heavenly father who has all the tomorrows in hand. Gladness and joy have returned to my home, and with it, a whole set of people I wouldn't have missed knowing for anything.

As a single woman in my fifties, I have two sets of friends. One group of women are my married friends. I value them like a traveler cherishes the memories of home. In their presence I am an expat in a foreign country who has encountered fellow citizens, and I long to discuss the familiar subjects that remind me of the days when my life in some ways mirrored theirs with the love, and security, *real or false,* and predictability that I once took for granted. We are born with the need to belong, for connection, and I revel in the steady atmosphere of their connectedness to the one person in life who still loves them "til death do us part." Contrary to what married people might think of divorced people, their friendship doesn't make us sad, it gives us hope, because with them we are reminded that love does indeed last.

The other group of women are my single friends, mostly divorced, who I love and treasure as a veteran who values his fellow soldiers who fought on different fronts in the same war and survived. We empathize together, cry together, pray the same prayers for our children, and mourn, *but not for too long*, the good days that preceded the bad ones, that preceded the battle we all fought and lost- because no one wins in divorce.

One thing I noticed before I was divorced was how some of the most godly women I knew suddenly talked like a sailor when the subject of their ex-husband came up in conversation. I would laugh uncomfortably not wanting to judge because I had not walked in their shoes *and had no intention too*. I had never had a foul mouth in my life. I said "gosh" one time as a kid and my brother told on me. I was marched straight to bathroom and a bar of soap was shoved into my mouth. I didn't say another cuss word for forty years. But upon leaving my attorney's office after signing the papers to serve my husband a few days after I had fled for my life, I surprised myself by saying a bad word on the phone with Mom when I called to tell her what had happened. To her credit, she made no reaction. Her silence told me she understood. She never knew what a comfort her small *non-gesture* was to me.

I now have many friends who have walked a similar journey as mine. When I meet someone new, I want to hear her story and find the thread that we all seem to have in common-how God has provided. God's provision looks different for everyone, but I am always amazed at how God works in each person's life post-divorce. How God provides financially, because usually that's the biggest worry. How God provides for the children, whether it's through counseling, or a relative or a family friend. And how God provides professionally or philanthropically or both. I love learning what each person finds to do that reconstructs her life now, making it meaningful, worth getting out of bed for, and applying the mascara.

Once I got over being ashamed of my new status, I began to invite people over to my apartment and later to my little cottage. This helped me ward off the loneliness that threatened to take me down every day for years. It was one of the worst parts of the aftermath of losing my family as I knew it. Having "life" happen in my home again not only gave me the chance to practice the hospitality I learned from Mom, but it provided another layer of purpose that I needed to help build what I came to call my "new life". Now, gathering my friends around my table or on my patio feeds me like nothing else, and is not only worth the effort, but what I learn during those visits is invaluable. These women are intelligent, creative, and brave. Many of them have found their voices again and are learning to use them for all kinds of good purposes. All my friends are better than me in areas I long to improve in; thus, I stay motivated to continue to grow and to learn to love more like Christ does.

If you have gotten this far in my story, I hope you'll pause to ponder these questions: How are you going to respond to what has happened to you? What do you want to look back on and say that you did? Who is your faith in?

I don't know your circumstances, but I know that really bad things can happen to people. Unfair, unjust, humiliating, beyond tragic things. Even so, there's one answer to the questions above that can start you on the journey to healing and recovery – Forgiveness. Maybe not today, maybe not tomorrow or next week, or even next year, but eventually the answer is to forgive. If we don't forgive, we are tethered to the perpetrator for the rest of our lives, and chances are we become one ourselves.

Forgiveness was God's answer to man's offense against Him. Instead of wiping us off the face of the earth, God came down to earth as a man so He could identify with us in our brokenness and heal us from the self-inflicted mortal wound of going our own way and rejecting his. In the most unjust sacrifice ever made God traded places with us. He took punishment and death, so we could have forgiveness and eternal life. And He offers this gift to you.

Take the gift. Accept His forgiveness. Receive His love. And you'll find that with it comes His presence that's more real than loneliness, and His peace that holds steady when all hell breaks loose, *as well as all the things you longed for in your marriage and never had.* Let Him start your story over. Let Him show you that the biggest miracles of all are the hidden ones that take place in the darkest recesses of your soul where your greatest pain cries out.

Will you take hold of the rope and start the climb? If you do, you'll find people along the way to hold you up when you're weary, to encourage when you're afraid, and to tell you the truth when the lies bombard you. But most importantly, if you don't take the rope, you'll never start the climb, and you'll never know what your new life could have been.

Follow Me...

Prayer to Break Bitter Root Judgments Expectancies and Inner Vows

Dear Heavenly Father:

I see that I sinned against You when:

1. **I got bitter toward**: _____

   For: _____

2. **Even worse I judged** _____ for what happened and in so doing I guaranteed that the negative seed I planted when I judged him/her would come back to me.

   Galatians 6:7 "Do not be deceived, God is not mocked; for whatever a man sows, this he will also reap."

3. **Still worse, I formed the conscious or unconscious expectancy That:** _____

Forgive me that I got bitter and that I judged _____,

and that I formed expectancies about: _____

Forgive me also for the following conscious or unconscious inner vows I made:

My expectancy is that: _____
(Example: Everyone is untrustworthy)

Therefore, I vow that: _____
(Example: I will never trust anyone, a man, a person in authority...)

You don't have to remember making the inner vow- you bear the bad fruit of it, so you know you did it.

Ask, **What bad fruit am I bearing now?** What has not gone we for me (jobs, relationships, mostly relationships) and **what ro have I played**?

(Not everyone plays a role in his/her suffering, there are compellir exceptions, but many people do.)

In the powerful name of Jesus, I now break the bitter-ro judgment I made and any conscious or unconscious expectancies formed. The foolish inner vows I made I now break in Jesus' name

I choose in Jesus name to forgive _____ who wronge me; and _____, who participated i that wrong.

I choose from this day forward to not hold anything against hin her/ them. **I set them free, and I cancel any debt I think they ow me**.

Please forgive me for any hardness of heart I formed when made the bitter-root judgments and inner vows toward _____

_____

By FAITH I ask You to take away my heart of stone and giv me a new heart as You promised in **Ezekiel 36:26.** (Part of th four Elements of the Promised Restoration – return from exil cleansing of sin, renewal of heart, enablement by God's Spirit to liv God's way)

"Moreover, I will give you a new heart and put a new spirit withi you; and I will remove the heart of stone from your flesh and **giv you a heart of flesh**." (Ezekiel 36:26)

Thank You that Your Word says in **Isaiah 61:1**

You came "to bind up the brokenhearted, to proclaim liberty t captives, and freedom to prisoners."

Your Word also says in **1 John 3:8**

The Son of God appeared for this purpose, to destroy the works of the devil."

Bitter-root judgments, expectancies, and foolish inner vows are the works of the devil.

Hebrews 12:15 "See to it that no one falls short of the grace of God and that no bitter root grows up to cause trouble and **defile many.**" I don't want the whole landscape of my life to be defiled by bitterness and unforgiveness.

Therefore, I put the cross of Jesus between me and the bitter-root judgments, expectancies, and inner vows that I've made. **The Cross now absorbs the consequences of my reaping and sowing. I now put all these things** (the bitter-root judgments, expectancies and inner vows) **under the blood of Jesus.**

Thank you, Lord, that I am now set free in Jesus' name. Please show me that I have a new heart in some specific way. I look forward to many positive results from praying this prayer. In Jesus name.

Once you have prayed this prayer, then there's the process of **walking it out.** When we are tested (encounter that person; a circumstance, or a memory that triggers bitterness or unforgiveness all over again...) after having "worked" the prayer we can boldly say, **"Show me the fruit Lord, You and I know that's not who I am anymore."**

Oswald Chambers:

If the Holy Spirit of God detects anything in you that is wrong, He does not ask you to put it right; He asks you to accept the light and He will put it right."

"You will never cease to be the most amazed person on earth at what God has done for you on the inside."

Made in the USA
Columbia, SC
06 May 2024

35222320R00072